This sixth issue of Tolka
published in Dublin in 2023

Text origination by Sarah McCoy
Page layout by Bartek Janczak
Printed by Creative Design & Print (creativedesignandprint.ie)

ISBN 978-1-739-8226-4-4

Tolka receives financial assistance from the Arts Council.

Anniversary hound, **Mollie Douthit,** oil on linen panel, 61x46cm, 2023.
Sara Baume's essay, 'The Lake House' (p. 1), is in response to this work.

The Lake Home

SARA BAUME

Mollie leaned over the kitchen sink and picked up a little glass bottle from the windowsill. She measured three drops into the plastic cap and showed me – it was viscous, dark brown – then she added a splash of water from the cold tap, and swirled, and held it out again so that I could see how the substance had turned – in a fraction of a second, in a spontaneous display of alchemy – so pale and cloudy that it resembled weak, milky tea. Then she knocked it down her throat like a shot, twisted her face in disgust and listed the names of the supplements she was taking to sustain her immune system. The sun was high above Mollie's cabin. Light reached in the kitchen window and across the sink, fingered the rug in front of the log stove and stopped. It was a peculiarly hot afternoon in May – the patch of sloping lawn outside the door was flecked with daisies. Further below I could see a billowing polytunnel and a stretch of meadow grass, and white bedsheets hanging on the washing line, glowing. But in the cabin it was shady and cool. Mollie spooned powdered Barleycup into two mugs and as the kettle boiled she told me what it contained – roasted grains and chicory root – because I had never tasted it before. All year, I had been visiting Mollie's paintings, the ones she called the lake home series. She would put them out for me, propped up against the wall and the legs of the workbench and the door of the fridge, lined up along the hard, narrow sofa, crowding her cramped living space. I always brought the dogs with me and I would grit my teeth as they snuffled around the canvasses and wagged their tails into the partially dried paint. I would try to shoo them away, but Mollie never seemed to mind. Nothing a little linseed can't fix, she would call out from the kitchen on the other side of the rug. The smell of scented candles, and of food, always filled the cabin – sandalwood, bergamot, fresh bread, toasted seeds, carrot soup with orange in it – and I often wondered if the paintings would look different without the attendant smells. I couldn't believe that Mollie had no protective feelings toward her work; it seemed rather that she was open to the influence of external forces, accepting of whatever it was that luck had in store. I would be apologetic, but secretly I liked the idea that a strand of hair would adhere itself to the surface of a canvas, leaving a surreptitious signature for a conservator of the future to peel off and ask herself: who was this dog? I had a tendency to search the surfaces of artworks for flaws; I found it exhilarating to locate a drip of coffee – it seemed to me as much a piece of biography as the painting itself.

We carried our mugs across the cabin and sat down on the carpet in front of the lake home series. Mollie broke a bar of dark pistachio-nut chocolate into shards inside its paper and I set the dictaphone app on my phone to record, placed it on the floor beside the chocolate, and then sampled the Barleycup – it tasted like hot, liquid bread. I always looked forward to meeting the paintings again – the one with the bat in the shower, the one with the big blue bed, the one with the tree that crawled with army worms, the one with two puppets hanging from their strings in a dark wardrobe, the one with a red staircase and an amorphous patch of black that intrigued me – a section that appeared to have been painted out and never painted over, to represent an absence and a presence simultaneously. The lake home had belonged to Mollie's grandparents and was where she, along with her parents and younger sister, had spent summers as a child in the 1980s and '90s. Her grandparents had bought it in the 1960s from a paraplegic Korean man, and so the house and garden had been designed to accommodate a wheelchair – the halls were wide, there was an abundance of bridges, the front pathway was a gently sloping zig-zag – and the design was distinctly influenced by East Asian culture – there was a rock garden, paper screen walls, and an extraordinary amount of red paint. Because Mollie had not yet made a painting of the façade, all year I had been trying to piece the house beside the lake in Minnesota together in my mind. The painting that came closest to an exterior view was mostly taken up by the olive-green carpet of a living room. It contained several well-spaced objects – an old-fashioned television set with rabbit-ears aerial, a tall lamp with a pleated shade, an inlaid coffee table and a bear skin mounted high above the sofa, legs splayed. A ladder led up to a mezzanine, where there were two single beds, a rug and a small, rectangular window that enclosed a patch of night sky, swimming with stars, a thumbnail Van Gogh. The downstairs windows were dark too, the wood-panelled walls sloped away from the carpet in every direction, and suddenly there were roof slates and the branches of a tree and an azure sky as if the room had been cracked open. It was night, I assumed, inside the lake house in Mollie's head, or night was its dominant feeling – safety, cosiness, portent – whereas outside it was always day, perhaps the sunny summer one upon which she arrived with her family each year, the lake shimmering into view between the trees through the car window. The first time I saw this painting, before I really looked, I took it to be a version of the cabin – the timber walls and ladder and mezzanine, the colours – and every time since I have continued to find it pleasingly confusing; the collision of past and present, of Minnesota and West Cork. It makes me wonder if, by becoming so attached to a place as a child, Mollie was unconsciously sentencing herself to seek it out again, later in life – had she moved all the way over here only to travel back in time?

In the months that I'd been visiting, the paintings of the lake home series had been changing, enigmatically. In the one with the yellow-headed bird, a vine of flowers had twined itself around the black railing – cat's ear, or lesser hawksbit, or dandelion – and an orb-shaped cloud had popped up in the sky. Mollie told me how, after she had painted the cloud, she had seen a white orb in her mind during a psychic meditation, hovering, bursting with light. She had a complex relationship with what she termed 'woo

woo' – as far as I could tell she was occasionally persuaded, and constantly bemused. She would try things out – psychics, healers, homeopaths – while simultaneously laughing at herself and her pursuit of eudemonia and transcendence. Even though I loved to hear her accounts of these sessions, I sensed it was only in my company that she joked, because I give the appearance of having no use for woo woo and she was instinctively cautious of being judged. I live a flatter life than Mollie; I experience less strong emotions, and this is a state I'm generally grateful for as well as, perhaps, the reason why I find her so fascinating. There were two new paintings positioned at a slight distance from the others – the first resembled the vertical view of a landscape, a satellite image. Here is the coastline, I guessed, tracing the tip of my finger through the air in front of the canvas, and a beach, and then the green and brown land. But no, the sea was a pond, she told me, the beach was a sandbox, the land was the deck of the lake home. The deck was red, she said, but it's brown, I said, and then Mollie explained *grounds* to me, how she builds colour in coats on the canvas as well as by mixing them on the palette. It influences the shade on top, she said, most of the paintings are yellow beneath the surface, or mossy green, and if there's any kind of gap it stops the stark white from peeking through. The red of the deck would be richer – righter – because there was brown beneath it. Looking at the just-begun painting I was struck by the bathos of sandboxes in suburban gardens, by the melancholy act of filling a little pit in a concrete yard with store-bought sand, clean as sugar, and handing a child a plastic spade and a castle-shaped bucket in order to simulate the experience of the tremendous, gorgeous, dangerous ocean. I asked Mollie if there was a shift between what the paintings looked like in her mind before she started work, and what they looked like in the real world, on the canvas, and she barked out a despairing laugh. Trying to align those two things is what the whole of painting boils down to, she said. It is the same trouble with sentences – I always know what I want to say but fashioning it into a string of words that I can type out with my fingers and see with my eyes – that is where the work of writing lies, the torture and the rapture.

The second of the new paintings depicted what looked like the inside of a dimly lit garden shed. On one side there was the edge of a frame and a slice of a pane of glass – it had a menacing atmosphere which would, I thought, have been lost if Mollie had chosen to paint the entirety of the window. I never think about composition, she whispered, things turn up in certain places of their own volition – before she even lifts a brush the paintings have already been abandoned to a certain degree of, again, luck, only this time it is the luck of internal forces. What is excluded is as important as what is included, and every painting is haunted by this process. That's why I like visiting them, I said, seeing what has materialised or dematerialised, picturing what they might finally become. Do you like the idea of what they *might be* better than what they *are*? Mollie asked, her tone somehow both anxious and provocative. NO, I yelped, I always trust what's there – your painted universe. I had thought that this was the answer she wanted, but instead she seemed crestfallen and started to talk about Hitchcock

– how much she admired his films and how little they are about him; how he had managed to generate this distance and yet still persuade so many people to appreciate his work. In the painting of the big blue bed she had included two of Alfred Hitchcock's dogs, one on each side – a white Sealyham terrier called Mr Jenkins and a black cocker spaniel called Edward IX. If my paintings are too personal, Mollie said, I'm afraid they won't let other people in.

My favourite painting in the lake home series is of an oval of lawn with pale tracks running all the way round. On one side of the lawn there's a tree with the roots exposed, a long, branchless trunk, a bulbous crown, and on the other side there's a huge, grey dog and its shadow. Features at the top and bottom of the canvas – stone paving, red railings – have been cropped from view. The dog is mythological in appearance, a version of Cúchulainn's wolfhound; in fact, it is a deerhound that Mollie knows personally. It belongs to the Ballydehob tree surgeon and wandered into the cabin one morning while his master was nearby, assessing an unwieldy copse. The first time I saw the painting I had commented in a throwaway manner that the snout was too short for a deerhound; Mollie did not reply but later the same week she sent me a photograph of the painted dog with a somewhat altered, longer snout, and I was moved. I find the paintings of the lake home series bizarre, and yet at the same time I always feel as if I am inside them, sifting through my own memory bank, clutching at familiarities. The painting of the oval lawn transports me to Iowa City, where I spent three months on a writing residency in 2015, having never been anywhere in America before, other than New York. The

Midwest was a revelation to me. Without any dogs to walk, first thing every morning I would get up and run – I have never been able to train myself to slow down and jog; I always sprint and quickly tire – around a nearby park that seemed colossal: the established trees and a sprawling network of tracks and a fat river that sawed a straight line. I was stunned by the quantity of open space and sky; it gave me a piercing understanding of the vastness of the continent; it made me realise that I live on a pokey island adjacent to a continent cluttered with pokey countries. What, I wondered, did America feel like for Americans – was its largeness perceptible; did the amount of sky seem ordinary? Though there is nothing specific about the lawn in Mollie's painting that makes it resemble the park in Iowa City, still I could not see it without remembering my mornings there, running laps so that I did not get lost, the desolation of being so small in such a large place.

Later on in the week, alone at my desk, I searched the internet for 'propolis', the only name I was able to remember of the supplements that Mollie had listed as she stood by her sink. It is, I discovered, a sticky matter harvested by bees from the buds of cone-bearing trees; the workers use it like glue to help build their hives, literally licking it onto the walls of the sheltering structure. It possesses all kinds of magical properties, healing skin and fighting bacteria, but for certain people it also carries 'the risk of bleeding', whatever that means, as if bleeding is not usually risky. I switched off the internet and started to play back the audio that I'd recorded in the cabin and realised at once that it had been a mistake to position the phone alongside the chocolate wrapper

– our conversation was periodically interrupted by the vociferous rustling of paper. I was surprised by the strength of Mollie's accent; to my naked ear she did not sound so American, and I was surprised again, and vaguely concerned, that I also sounded American – sometimes it would take a few seconds before I was able to identify whose voice was whose. I have a very soft lisp – sustained from breaking my jaw in a bike accident in my twenties – that suddenly sounded monstrous. Mollie and I paused to sip our Barleycups and nibble on the chocolate as we talked; we intermittently hooted with laughter. As I listened, alone at my desk, I was suddenly ambushed by the awful and specific fear that none of it was of any consequence, actually – the practices to which we separately, assiduously devoted our days; the things she painted, the things I wrote, our repetitive, sheltered, privileged lives – then a strimmer kicked off in the background, the racket of a spinning line savaging the meadow grass, shooting out severed flower heads, and our voices were chewed up by the noise.

A Man in Fragments

EM CIORAN

FROM *NOTEBOOKS*, TRANSLATED BY PATRICK JAMES ERRINGTON

Translator's Note

The following is an excerpt from Notebooks, the first English translation of EM Cioran's *Cahiers*, collected after his death by his long-time partner Simone Boué and published in the original French by Gallimard in 1997. Gathering into a single volume the thirty-four journals filled between 1957 and 1972, *Notebooks* is less a diary than an exercise book, a collection of attempts, attacks, failures and flailings that would lead to the famous French works like *History and Utopia* and *The Trouble with Being Born* (all translated by the late Richard Howard). Selected here are entries spanning 1959 to 1963, providing the first glimpses in the English language of the man behind the philosopher: the sleepless nights and chance encounters, the paralysing torments of a mind that finds itself unwillingly, unbearably and beautifully human. *Notebooks* by EM Cioran, translated by Patrick James Errington, is forthcoming with New York Review Books.

In memoriam Richard Howard

From disquiet to disquiet, from disease to disease – where am I going? This feeling of radical helplessness in the face of everything. Born defenceless.

Evil, just like Good, is a creative force. Of the two, though, Evil's the more active. All too often, Good is on welfare.

There was a time when I wouldn't spend a single day without several hours listening to music, without reading a single poem. Now prose takes the place of everything. What decline, what degradation!

Neutralise the effects of Creation.

The most minor act represents to me the problem of all acts; living, for me, becomes Life – which complicates breathing to the brink of breathlessness.

I am a writer who doesn't write. This sense of surrendering my nights, my 'destiny', of betraying it, of wasting my hours.

Oppression. Certainty of being an unnamed.

If I make no progress along any plan, if I produce nothing, it's because I seek what cannot be found, what we, at one point, called Truth. Not being able to attain it, I pace, I wait, I wait . . .

I am an *irrepressible* skeptic.

I can no longer recall who defined themselves thus: 'I am the site of all my states.' The definition suits me completely, almost exhausts my entire nature.

Slept in the afternoon. Upon waking, for a second I felt what the dead feel. The dazzling enlightenment of a corpse.

If, every day, I had the courage to howl for a quarter hour, I would enjoy perfect sanity.

All my 'writings' are nothing, in the end, but an exercise of anti-utopia.

When anyone suggests to me to ignore a grudge, I always have the urge to slap them, to show just how wrong they are.

All considered, life is an extraordinary thing.

There is nothing more disappointing, more fragile and more false than a brilliant mind. Seek instead the boring ones; they *respect* banality – what is eternal in things or in ideas.

I don't understand X: he is somehow boring without being banal. Boredom is what emerges from the search for originality, from the pursuit of the unusual, that permanent and useless surprise.

There's nothing worse than a thinker who believes it is his duty to explain everything, who buries every problem in words. Volubility

– a sin against the spirit. Even the greatest have not escaped it.

A god begins to become *false* the moment no one is willing to die for him.

Prayer bursts from my state of depression which exults.

A religion is finished the moment it no longer gives birth to heresies.

What has falsified everything is our historical culture. We no longer wonder about God, but about *forms* of god; about religious sensibility and experience, not the *object* that justifies either.

This afternoon, wanting to write about glory but finding nothing to say, I went to lie down. So often my great enterprises drive me to bed, that pathetic terminus of my ambitions.

Nothing hinders the continuity of thinking so much as feeling the physical presence of the brain. This is perhaps why the mad think only in flashes.

It was the desire for glory that ruined paradise. Any time we want to escape anonymity, this symbol of contentedness, we give in to the suggestion of the serpent.

I value nothing as much as a skeletal prose shot through with a shiver.

Poetry *properly speaking* seems more and more inconceivable to me; I can only bear now that which is implicit, indirect, that which is precisely *not spoken* – a poetry without the methods and subterfuges it's usually comprised of.

Originality is incompatible with 'good taste', the prerogative and curse of ancient civilisations.

There is no genius without a strong dose of bad taste.

X – I admire him because he does not realise just how ridiculous he is.

To *perish*! This word I love so, and which, curiously enough, doesn't suggest to me anything irrevocable.

To have 'taste' is to give in to the conventional and to delicately relish mediocrity.

To oppose great taste, taste from 'on high', in Hugo's magnificent phrase.

Midnight. I should spend my life alone, reflecting ceaselessly on Time.

Accidentally ran into X – always this perplexing combination of scoundrel and madman, but at the core utterly elusive: a man who does not have even a notion of 'veracity', someone physiologically 'inexact' and amoral. His great excuse is the universal contempt he has managed to arouse around him. There is something of the serpent in him. I have always felt a sense of disgust – and curiosity – about him. Terror, too, in front of this slithering creature, unease at his appearance. Cold, glittering eyes; there is metal in his gaze. In his blood there must be some mix of Greek and Slavic, two irreconcilable elements that could only give birth to a monster. Subterranean and arrogant. An impression of vertigo. His obsequiousness, monumental. All this, however, includes a few gifts. When I met him for the first time, not having read anything of his, I said to M.: 'He must have talent. He's so dreadful.' Dreadful both morally and physically.

Wrote one day about him: 'Portrait of a snake'.

P.S. These notes are so stripped of mercy that I am ashamed. Pity, in my case, follows disgust: Oh, how beings hurt me!

Still on the subject of X – What he is, the phenomenon he embodies, is only conceivable in a country like ours, where the disparate ethnic imports have not been consolidated, melted, mixed organically, where the blood is, as they say, uncultivated because 'culture' has not done its individualising and leveling work. Him, he is the monster in its natural, uncorrected state. His cunning, his deceptiveness – which are immense – are completely lacking 'varnish', he is hypocrisy . . . unveiled, the imposter in full daylight, the repugnant spotlit, and this precisely because of his continuous and *obvious* dissimulation. One is struck by his total insincerity, perceivable in every gesture, in every word; but that's not the right word, since being insincere is to hide the truth, or some calculation or God knows what; but he who hides all hides nothing; for he has no veracity in him, no criterion by which he acts or judges. There is in him only an enormous obstinacy, a vile voraciousness, a thirst for gain and fame of the most vulgar degree. He's scum, a fanatic without belief, an *intentional* madman . . .

Vulgarity is contagious, always; delicacy, never.

Pain is a feeling; suffering, a sentiment. One cannot say: a feeling of suffering.

Great character is not open but closed; its force resides in its refusal, its *massive* refusal.

In all defeat, in the slightest symptom of disappearance, there is a touch of delight.

Is pleasure a form of disintegration?

All sensuality is pain. A special pain, to be fair.

My joys are all latent sorrows.

Albert Camus was killed in a car accident. He died at the moment when everyone, and maybe he too, knew that he had nothing more to say and that by living he would only fall from his disproportionate, abusive, even ridiculous glory. Enormous sorrow upon learning of his death, yesterday evening, at 11 p.m., in Montparnasse. An excellent minor writer, but who achieved greatness by having been completely free from vulgarity, despite all the honours that were heaped on him.

X: he is interested in everything, which explains his obvious weakness ... Attracted to the accessory, to the 'living', he passes by the essential, he no longer knows what is important above all else. A painful and universal dispersal.

I spoke to Camus only once, in 1950, I think. I've said so many ill things about him, and now I feel a terrible and inexplicable remorse. I lose all my capacities when confronted with a corpse, especially one so respectable. A sadness without name.

Justice is, *literarily* speaking, a mediocre ideal.

Wherever I go, the same feeling of unbelonging, of playing some useless and idiotic game, a falseness, not on the part of others but on my own; I feign interest in what barely matters, I play a role constantly, out of cowardice, to save face; but I am not *in* it, since what is close to my heart is *elsewhere*. Cast out of paradise, *where* will I find my place, where will I find a home? Fallen, a million times fallen. There is in me like a hosannah struck down, hymns reduced to powder, an explosion of regret.

A man for whom there is no homeland on earth.

Grappling with the French language: an agony in the truest sense of the word, a struggle in which I am always on the losing side.

All that is civilisation is *derived*, and all that is derived is worthless.

History, in whatever form we envisage it, is a screen that hides the absolute.

The *original* alone is true. All that the mind invents is false.

I have lost a number of my old faults; in exchange, I have acquired others. Equilibrium remains intact.

Don't waste your time criticising others, censuring their works; make your own, devote all your hours to it. The rest is clutter or infamy. Be true to what is true in yourself, what is 'eternal' even.

If you judge your contemporaries without pity, you run the risk of being right and appearing to posterity as an incisive and clairvoyant mind. But, at the same time, you give up the adventurous side of admiration, and the welcome errors it entails. Yes, admiration is an adventure, all the more beautiful because it's almost always wrong. It's frightening, though reasonable, to have no illusions about anyone.

There is nothing more lamentable than to be inescapably right.

(On the subject of the moralists who fell precisely into this trap.)

No kind of literary originality is possible while respecting syntax. We must wreck the sentence if we want to pull anything out of it.

The thinker alone must adhere to the old superstitions, to clear language and common syntax. It's because originality at its very base has the same demands as in the days of Thales.

Heraclitus, Pascal, the first even more fortunate than the second, because only fragments of his work remain. How lucky they were not to have to organise their interrogations into a system! The commentator has a field day – anyone who likes filling in the gaps, the intervals between the 'thoughts' or the maxims; who likes wandering with impunity; he can, without much risk, construct any figure he pleases. Since what he loves is arbitrariness, which gives him the illusion of liberty and invention: a cheap rigor.

Asked to write an article on Camus. I refused. His death devastated me, but I can find nothing to say about an author who had his fill of glory, and whose work, as I said in my letter of abstention, is of 'desperately evident significance'.

Camus, who protested so much against injustice, should have done so against that of his own glory, if he wanted to be consistent with himself. But that would have been indecent. And he undoubtedly believed that his glory was earned.

If we were to push the mania for justice to the limit, we would fall into ridicule or destroy ourselves. There is more elegance in resignation than in revolt, and more beauty in anonymity than in the noise and uproar around a name.

Anyone who adheres to their own celebrity is despicable, anyone who is neither humiliated nor disgusted by it.

As lonely as a God on welfare.

In my view, negation carries such prestige that, in cutting me off from all other things, it has made me narrowminded, stubborn, and crippled. As some live under the spell of 'progress', I live under the spell of No. And all the while I understand that one can say yes, agree to everything, though such a feat, which I recognise in others, requires of me a leap of faith that I don't now feel capable of. It's that No has entered my bloodstream, having already perverted my mind.

There is something nauseating and gruelling about the use of an abstract style: all these empty words juxtaposed to convey the unreal, which we call thought.

Oh! how I would love to confine myself to sensation alone, to a world before the concept, to the infinitesimal variations of a felt impression which I would have to render in a thousand astonishing, unactionable words. To write the *sense* directly, becoming an interpreter of the body and uncoordinated soul! To transcribe only what I see, what touches me, doing what a reptile would do if put to work – not a reptile, an insect, since a reptile has that unfortunate reputation of being intellectual. The book would be poetic *by pure physiology*.

I have read the classics too much to ever return to *the origins*, to go by means of language beyond language.

James Joyce: the most prideful man of the century. Because he wanted, and in part attained, the impossible, with the stubbornness of a mad god. And because he never compromised with the reader and did not try to be readable at all costs. Culminating in obscurity.

To succeed in abolishing the public, in passing beyond it, in counting on no one, in swallowing up the universe.

What ruins most talents is that they do not know how to limit themselves.

Nothing sterilises a writer so much as the pursuit of perfection. To produce, one needs to give in to one's nature, abandon the self, listen to the voices . . . eliminate the censorship of irony or *good* taste . . .

Everything I have that is *good* comes from my laziness; without it, what would have stopped me enacting my evil plans? It has fortunately contained me within the limits of 'virtue'.

All our vices come from an excess of activity, from this propensity to *archieve*, to give an honorable appearance to our shortcomings.

I have never spoken or written the word *solitude* without feeling a shudder of pleasure.

Articles *on*, studies, books *on*, always on someone, on authors, on works, on the ideas of others; amplified reports, useless and mediocre commentaries; no matter how remarkable, it would never change the thing. Nothing personal, nothing original; everything derived. Oh! it is better to speak about oneself with nonsense than about others with talent. An idea that is not lived, that does not spring from the source, is worth nothing. What a nauseating sight, this humanity of borrowing, so cerebral, learned, living as a parasite on the mind.

The historian of philosophy is not a philosopher. A concierge who asks himself questions, on the other hand, is.

Concerning invention, man should have stopped with the wheelbarrow. Any technical improvement is harmful and should be denounced as such. One could say the only meaning of 'progress' is to contribute to an increase in noise, to the consolidation of hell.

I swear to never speak of things that I know little about, not to improvise for anything in the world, not to be unworthy of the subject I am treating, never to bring myself into disrepute my own eyes.

(Oath taken upon leaving one of M's lectures, a particularly superficial one.)

The *Mass in B minor*. Nearly three years since I lost touch with music. I was dead; Bach has resurrected me.

My tastes tend toward shortcuts, toward compressed forms, toward those funerary inscriptions in the *Anthology*.

I am not a writer. I don't find words that fit to what I feel, to what I endure. 'Talent' is the ability to fill in the gap between experience and language. For me, that gap is there, gaping, impossible to fill or close up. I live in automatic sadness, I am an elegiac robot.

Negation for me has never come from reasoning, but from a sort of primordial desolation – the arguments come *after*, to back it up. Every *no* is therefore a no of the blood.

Lady Macbeth, Madame de Brinvilliers – women after my own heart. If feel, in in moments of deep despondency, a kind of longing for cruelty.

Yesterday evening, before sleeping, I saw with hallucinatory precision the Earth reduced to a simple point, taking, so to speak, zero dimensions, and I understood, what I have always known, that it is useless and ridiculous to writhe and suffer, to write above all, in such a minuscule and such an unreal space. To devote oneself to doing – to *be* at all – one mustn't have this fatal capacity to make oneself external to one's actions, to place oneself by thought beyond the planet, beyond the universe itself.

I value a mind only insofar as it does not fit with its time, just as I only admire those who desert their time, or rather: those who are traitors to time and to history.

The angel of the Apocalypse does not say 'There is no more time', but rather 'There is no more delay.'

I have always lived with the feeling that time is being eaten away from within, that it's about to wear out its possibilities, that it lacks *duration*. And this failing, that is its failing, has filled me with satisfaction and with dread.

(to comment)

Cured of my anxiety, I wouldn't even have the consistency of a ghost.

When one isolates life from matter and contemplates it in its pure state, so to speak, one can better perceive its exceptional fragility: a 'construction' in the air, out of kilter, without anchor point, without any trace of reality.

And it is no doubt because I have too often pulled it from its base so as to look it head-on, face-to-face, that I myself have to come have nothing to anchor me, nothing to hold on to.

Everything that keeps me from working seems good to me, and every moment offers so many ways out.

If I examine myself without any complacency, it is a flight from responsibility, a fear of taking on even the tiniest one, that seems to me my dominant natural trait. I'm a deserter in my soul. And it is not for nothing that I see abandonment, in everything, as the hallmark of wisdom.

Someone quite correctly defined sadness as 'a kind of twilight that follows pain'.

Anxiety, which treats the possible as déjà-vu, is it not a kind of *memory of the future*?

To say that I regret everything is an understatement; I am a walking regret, and nostalgia devours my blood and devours itself. There is no remedy on earth for what I suffer, only poisons to make it more active and intolerable. How I blame civilisation for having discredited tears. Having unlearned how to cry, we are all helpless, riveted to our dry eyes.

To seek *being* with words! Such is our quixotism, such is the delirium of our essential enterprise.

If ever mortal was tormented, *flayed* by self-doubt, it is me. In everything. When I give a text to a journal, my first thought is to take it back, to change it, and above all to abandon it. I have no faith in anything I have done or thought. And if I have one certainty, it is my distrust of myself, which calls into question not only my capabilities, but the very foundations and reason of my being. I am literally *armed* with misgivings. How under these conditions could

I undertake anything? How, with so many doubts, could I decide on even the smallest act, the smallest thought?

I was made for insignificance and frivolousness, and sufferings have melted over me and condemned me to seriousness, for which I have zero talent.

Outside of extreme solitude, when we our reduced entirely to ourselves, we live false identities, we are false.

Every moment I'm not thinking about death, I feel like I am cheating, tricking *someone* in me.

When I'm out walking and I look at passersby, I feel so distant from them that it is like they remind me of a nightmare I had in another life. Literally and figuratively, no other denomination suits nor flatters me so much as that of *stranger*. I was not made to have a nationality. Whether I lost mine or never had one, it's clear that Fate decided thus.

I became so interested in style it is because I saw it as a challenge to nothingness; unable to get on with the world, I had to get on with the word.

Nothing more degrading than the daily return of those same stupid obsessions that disgrace us in our own eyes. Their frequency, their regularity, there is no choice but to interpret them as some kind of punishment; otherwise, we'd die of shame.

Nostalgia and anxiety – that is what my 'soul' is reduced to. Two abysses; the past and the future. Between them, just enough air to breath, just enough space to stand in.

Civilisation would be ignoble if it weren't doomed.

He stopped writing; he had nothing left to hide.

A writer's heritage is his secrets, his crushing and unspoken defeats; and it is the fermentation of his shames that guarantees his fertility.

The whole 'mystery' of life lies in our attachment to life, in the almost miraculous mental fog that keeps us from discerning our own precarity and illusions.

It was Sieyès, if I'm not mistaken, who said that we must be drunk or mad to believe that it's possible to express anything in our known languages.

Writers – I can read only the really unwell, those whose ailments *light up* every page, every line. I like health *willed*, not inherited or acquired.

When I write, as soon as I stop attacking and cursing, I become bored and I put down the pen.

Sometimes I have to ask myself if, outside of my frenzies, I really exist. They abandon me and I vegetate, dragging myself along like an old rag.

All that frightens me stimulates me.

Death of N. J. H. – it is impossible to 'assimilate' the death of a friend. It is a piece of news that remains on the outside of our spirit, that cannot enter, but which seeps slowly into the heart, an almost unnoticed grief.

Each death calls everything into question, forcing us to resume as if beginning our lives all over again.

The Spanish have heart, like all cruel peoples . . .

The incredible indiscretion of death . . .

The belief in the irreality of the world does not cancel out fear.

For some – and I count myself among them – to be separate from Spain is to separate from oneself.

There is in me a longing for something that does not exist in life, nor even in death – a desire that nothing on earth satisfies, except certain moments when music evokes the heartbreak of another world.

Impossible to sleep. Everything hurts. My body! I managed to go outside: it seems like it is the first time I have looked at the stars like this, without a single hope or regret. Absolute perception without thinking, probably out of fear of thinking of the drama playing out in my bones, out of fear too of breaking forever with the day.

Demented morning; a sense of sudden poisoning. I stepped out into the street; impossible to look anyone in the eye; at the pharmacy, I could not stop myself making some hurtful remark to the teller. Raging against the whole world, a desperate, useless fury. Feeling as though there is venom in the veins, as though having gone further than any other demon.

To be able to rein myself in, I would need several centuries of English education – but I come from a country where we howl at funerals.

In the mountains near Santander, in the middle of a superb countryside, were cows that had a certain sadness about them, according to my friend Nunez Morante.

'Why would they be?' I asked him. 'They have everything I dream of: silence, sky . . .'

'They are sad to be, *por ser*,' he replied.

He was the one who said to me the other day something that could very well be true: 'The worker does not want to improve his condition, he wants to *command*.'

Also in the Santander mountains, a little lost village. In the pub, a few shepherds started to sing. In Western Europe, Spain is the last country that still has soul.

All the exploits and failures of Spain have translated into song. Its own secret: nostalgia *as knowledge*, a science of regret.

An English journalist called me the other day to ask my opinion about *God and the twentieth century*. I was about to go to the shop, I told him, adding that I was not of the requisite disposition to discuss such a preposterous problem. The further we go, the more our problems deteriorate and take on the mask of the whole era.

Chekhov: the most hopeless writer of all time. During the war, I lent his books to Picky P., gravely ill, who begged me not to give him any more, because with nothing to do but read them, he was losing the courage to resist his illness.

My *Précis*: the world of Chekhov degraded into essay.

My whole life I have always been in love with bad weather. Clouds reassure me; when, in the morning, from my bed, I see them passing, I feel the strength to face the day. But the sun, I could never handle it; I have not enough light in me to get along with it. It only awakens, stirs up my shadows. Ten days of blue skies puts me in a state neighbouring madness.

All men want to be what they are not. I dreamt of action in my youth; then, philosophy. I mistook delirium for action, and despair for thought. What am I good for? Looking and moping, waiting for the hours to burst.

In the hotel, I lived for fifteen years in a garret; it's still a garret that I now occupy in an 'apartment'. I have always lived right below the roof. I am a *man of the final floor*, a man of the eaves.

Dinners in the city – what a waste! Impossible to work the next day. One keeps the echo of words that we had or overheard. One chews all day over all the patterns of frenetic and useless conversation. Thus is born the habit of digression, this stain on the intellect.

Everything's telling me to abandon the game, but I don't *want* to, I persist.

Delusional pity; I imagine all suffering down to the mineral.

Write a 'Metaphysics of Goodbye'.

Stepping into sleep as though it were an abattoir.

I quit smoking for two weeks. Two weeks of torture. From now on I will be more lenient toward the 'intoxicated'.

I have taken up smoking again . . . The shame!

No writer accepts even the slightest restriction on what he creates. He has too many self-doubts to be able to face the doubts that others have about him.

I have never written a single line without *afterward* feeling some kind of embarrassment, an intolerable discomfort, without radically doubting my capacities and my 'mission'. No clear-sighted person should take up a pen – unless they like to torture themselves. Self-confidence is as good as possessing 'grace'. God help me to believe in myself. Wouldn't *conversions* come from the impossibility of enduring lucidity for one more moment? Are they not a result of tormented souls – of the too-frequent self-reflection? The hell of knowing *oneself*, which neither the oracle nor Socrates could have predicted.

All solitude is too small, to me, even that of the great Void, even that of God. What terrible demand has crept itself into my longings?

Stop all desires! That is my aim, my absolute *desire*!

Heard on the radio some Hungarian Gypsy music. It's been years since I've heard it. Heartbreaking vulgarity. Memories of nights drinking in Transylvania. The immense boredom that pushed me to drink with anyone. Deep down, I'm a 'sentimentalist', like all those central European types.

I wandered around the fifth arrondissement. Rue Rataud, where Eveline lived, rue Lhomond, where I lived for a month in 1935, and then all these old roads that remind me of my 'youth'. Rue Pot-de-Fer, rue Amyot, the end of the rue Cardinal-Lemoine, etc. Funeral march: I carried mourning of my spirit.

Birthday present: the old idea of suicide has taken hold of me again for some time, and has seized me particularly hard *today*. React, keep on your feet . . .

I think of Sibiu, the city I loved most in the world, and of the terrible crises of boredom that I experienced there. Sunday afternoons when I would haunt the deserted streets, or perhaps alone in the forest or in the fields . . . If I so miss these moments, it is because of their *setting*. I am a provincial at heart.

I quit smoking again. That night, I awoke with such a hatred of tobacco that upon rising I destroyed my last pack of cigarettes, the cigarette holder, and the entire little arsenal of the most grotesque intoxication there is.

There's no point trying break a habit by will alone; it's the saturation point, it's the disgust and exasperation that are the root of dishabituation. We triumph only over that which we hate, after having loved.

. . . If I persist here on earth, it is because my horror of the world is insufficiently and incompletely sincere.

Having felt the feeling of being nothing, how can one wish to continue to be something? I have found no book with an argument that holds even the least bit against the evidence of the inanity of the universe.

What saves men, is that they do not know how little they are. Curse or privilege, I have always felt to the point of vertigo my own irreality, and that of everything else.

Sadness, which has for me become a permanent state, is the great obstacle to my 'salvation'. As long as it persists and I can't shake it off, I will remain nailed down to the miseries here on earth. Such is the paradox of sadness: it plunges us into this world at the same time as it separates us from it. It is complacency in heartbreak and in inconsolation.

In this universe where living is out of place.

On a bench, a man, vaguely 'foreign', embarrassed and sniggering, and a woman looking tense, devastated. I heard, as I passed in front of them, her say to him: 'It's finished.'

It's exactly the word I expected from her face.

From the time when I travelled France by bicycle and I would go rambling for months, I recall that my greatest pleasure was stopping in countryside cemeteries to smoke . . .

I have more than a talent, I have an instinct for regret.

I do not think there has ever been a man more intrinsically alone than me.

Nostalgia – balm and poison of my days. I literally dissolve into elsewhere. God knows what paradise I long for. Within me is the melody, the rhythm of the *Outcast*, and I spend my time humming my despair and my exile here on earth.

If one could go mad from the pure, 'logical', unfolding of sadness, I would have lost reason ages ago.

If suffering is the essence of existence, why have so few tried to escape it, why is the quest for salvation so rare? The essence of existence is the *attachment* to existence, which is to say existence itself. That this attachment leads ultimately to suffering – everyone agrees but no one wants to accept the consequences. At the core, the cry of humanity is, 'Suffering over deliverance!' Suffering, after all, is still part of existence, while deliverance is just empty bliss.

Paradox without name: I am trying to concoct an essay on . . . glory, and at the very moment when my uselessness, my weakness, and my degradation have reached their maximum point, when I have exhausted all possibility of despising myself, when, in sum, I have rejected myself and treat myself as undesirable.

One shouldn't sign what one writes. When you seek truth, what does a name matter? In the end, all that counts is anonymous poetry and thought, the creations of what we have called the 'eras of sincerity', before literature.

Only minor writers worry all the time about the destiny of their *œuvre*. Every book is perishable; only the pursuit of the essential is not.

The tragedy of human things evaporates as soon as we see it from a little distance. In truth, there is no tragedy except for the man in action.

I switch tables, chairs, rooms every five minutes – OK, let's be generous, every hour – as if I were seeking an *ideal* place to work, since whatever place I'm in never seems right; this ridiculous anxiety saddens me more than I can say. It has come to this, Lord!, and in an age where others throw themselves with joy into long-term enterprises! Better to die than continue like this.

When one no longer believe in love, one can still love, just as one can fight without convictions. However, in either case, something is broken. A building whose cracks stand in for style.

No subject seems to me important enough for me to take the trouble to treat it. This comes from an infirmity of my mind, which, for want of a better word, I'll call 'hopeless frivolity'. To come to this point, to this impossibility of focusing, and yet at the same time offering all the symptoms of gravely afflicted obsessive, it's to be completely unable to escape from a small circle, always the same one, the of precisely the same *subjects*!

Remorse is my vitality, my great resource.

In philosophy, as in everything, originality can be reduced to incomplete definitions.

Every original view is a partial view, voluntarily insufficient.

I know that all is unreal, but I do not know how to prove it.

Sensations of an elegiac assassin.

Renounce everything, even the role of the spectator.

I don't understand how one can write a book, any book – and yet . . .

There comes a time when we can no longer sacrifice ourselves to the inessential, and writing is reduced to chore, an ordeal even.

Sunday. Unable to sleep, I rose around 5.30 a.m. Wandering around the Luxembourg. There is but one pure light: that of the morning. As it advances through the day, the light prostitutes itself.

For five days, I have been taking a cure at Enghien. My nerves cannot handle it. Insomnia. The slightest remedy demolishes me. To cure oneself is to make oneself sick in another way.

At the core, only a pathetic tone suits me. As soon as I try another, I get bored and abandon my pen.

Silly me, I should have long ago converted myself to some earthly nonsense, and thus put a line under my existence, finished myself off.

My mind is not at the level of my sensitivity.

No matter how I try to get away from myself, my ailments bring me inescapably back. The ache of always meeting myself, the ache of identity – how well I know it!

Napoleon, on Saint Helena, from time to time would leaf through a grammar book . . . In that, at least, he proved that he was *French*.

I find myself unable to write. The Word is a wall I batter against, which resists me, which rises up in front of me. All the same, I know very well what I want to speak about, I *possess* my subject, I can see the design in the ensemble. But it is the expression that defeats me – nothing will surmount the barrier of the Verb. Never have I felt a paralysis like this, which affects me to the point of despair and, worse, to disgust. For six months I have smeared paper without ever writing one single page that doesn't bring me shame. I will never read another line of Hindu philosophy – it was the meditation on 'the renunciation of the fruit of action' that has led me here. If I had performed even any action at all! My abdication, alas! precedes even my desires!

To do anything, I must give up imposing upon myself any type of wisdom. I cannot fight forever against my nature. I am violating it stupidly, uselessly, wanting to be a sage. I was made to unleash myself, not vanquish myself.

It is my destiny to be only half-fulfilled. Everything, for me, is *truncated*: my way of being as much as my way of writing. A man in fragments.

An Interview with Sinéad Gleeson

HILARY A WHITE

Sinéad Gleeson's debut essay collection, *Constellations*, won Non-Fiction Book of the Year at the 2019 Irish Book Awards and the inaugural Dalkey Literary Award for an emerging writer. It was part of a cultural moment in which brave and bold non-fiction written by women (see Emilie Pine's *Notes to Self* and Doireann Ní Ghríofa's *A Ghost in the Throat*) seemed woven through a period of great social change in Ireland.

In May of this year, it was revealed that the award-winning writer, poet and anthologist was set to publish *Hagstone*, her debut novel, in spring 2024. Sinéad and I had crossed paths on the arts journalism circuit, and I had attended one of her essay-writing workshops. As a great many people will have experienced, she has been very supportive of my own tenuous beginnings in writing. We arranged a chat over Zoom about *Hagstone*, the writing life and her transition from non-fiction to fiction.

Hilary White (HW): When I saw there was an island setting in *Hagstone*, I immediately thought of 'Islanded', your essay in the *Women on Nature* anthology about the artists' retreat you attended on the Aran Islands.

Sinéad Gleeson (SG): I can't believe you remember that.

HW: My memory is funny. I don't remember what I had for breakfast but I definitely remember that essay, probably because I have connections to the west of Ireland. There's a real heaviness to the landscape that you capture, but you also reference strange sounds emanating from it, which appears to be a motif in *Hagstone* as well. Was the germ of the novel found on that trip?

SG: This book predates *Constellations* by a long way. I had bits and scraps and pieces of it, but you need a lot more focus for a novel. You need to have bunker time and away time, and, as you know, that's very hard to do when you're freelancing in the arts, when you've got children. I never found a run of time that would require that engine you need for a novel. It's also the capaciousness of it – it's very hard to keep a 300-page book in your head. When one essay isn't working, you can go and work on another. Did I start with the island? In a way, but the thing that the book actually started with was a sound. I remember one holiday, we were staying in Cork and I was making my husband drive a hundred kilometres because I'd heard that there was a phenomenon, this sound that happened in this place in Kerry. I've become really interested in who can hear things, why people hear things, and that idea of hearing the supernatural is really interesting to me. I wrote a little bit about that in *Constellations* ['The Haunted Haunting Women']. And, also, I'm married to a composer and sound engineer, and his ears are his tools. He'll ask me to listen to things that he's mastering, and I just simply can't hear the things that his ears can. So, it started with this sound which was quite mysterious that some could hear and some couldn't. And it was always going to be on an island, somewhere remote, and while I do draw very heavily on the West – it's very clearly based on an amalgamation of the Aran Islands, Inishbofin and Arranmore – I didn't want it to be any one of those places. It's also a much bigger island than any we have in Ireland, and I was reading work by Amy Liptrot or Malachy Tallack and thinking about Orkney and Shetland and places like that. Because of the story, it had to be a place that's not easy to get away from. It's maybe not an easy place to go back to either.

HW: In 'Islanded', you mention how James Joyce 'keenly felt a mysticism, Celtic or otherwise, that comes with the logistics, the location, the isolation of the people on these isles'. This feeling that they're at a slight remove to everything else.

SG: I spent a few days on the Aran Islands for that residency – it should have been a month but I couldn't get away for that long with family commitments. I talked to so many people on the island about what it was like. How do you get a car on to the island?

What do you do when the boats don't come in? Does everybody know everybody else? I found that sense of community fascinating, but also that sense of claustrophobia, which is a huge part of the book as well. Any place you can't quickly and expeditiously escape from is always interesting to me. In Ireland, we romanticise these places, but I imagine it's very, very hard to live somewhere like that. There's only so much looking at the sea and the cliffs you can do.

HW: From the synopsis, it almost sounds like there is a *Wicker Man*/folk-horror vibe to the novel – an outsider encountering a cult in an insular community.

SG: I always had the island, the sound, the main character. The Inions came a lot later. And like all those great moments, you don't have them very often and it's usually when you're doing something utterly banal. In my case, I was hanging out the washing and I had this very striking visual image of all of these women. I won't say too much about it but their arms were linked and I just thought to myself, *Who are these women?* I came in straight away and started writing about who they might be. I didn't even know what the scene was. I was going, *Where is that coming from?*

HW: You must have some idea.

SG: I've always been interested in our traditions and folklore, and studied history as the other half of my degree. I'm forever picking up books about the history of trees, myths, rituals. I don't know if you know Stephen Ellcock, who is a visual curator and publishes collections of photographs. Every time he publishes a new book, it's as if he's climbed into my brain and filled the book with all the kind of stuff that interests me: mythology; spiritualism; costumes; the occult; the planets; Surrealist painters, particularly channelled through artists like Hilma af Klint, Leonora Carrington, Ana Mendieta and Dora Maar. In my novel, because Nell is an artist, there are a lot of references to other artists, and I actually think the work of Irish female cubists like Mainie Jellett, Eva Hone and Mary Swanzy echo around the book too. I've been told it's a very visual book, and the influences extend to film, so of course things like *The Wicker Man*, *The Witch* and *Midsommar* hover over it, but that's more tonally than thematically. I wouldn't have called it a horror book by any stretch. I recently saw the brilliant Cornish film *Enys Men*, directed by Mark Jenkin, and got such a jolt as so much of it seemed to be in conversation with *Hagstone*. So many aspects of Irish culture fascinate me too – the rituals of Wren boys, changelings, banshees, sheela na gigs and how, despite how repressive and Catholic Ireland became for centuries, these very tribal, ancient and often transgressive interests survive. The fact that you'll still find farmers who won't cut down trees or build near fairy forts, and that it's not considered weird or supernatural here because it links back in many ways to who we used to be as a people before colonisation. I also read a lot of sci-fi, horror – not just literary stuff when I was younger – graphic novels, I was into all that kind of stuff. No more than yourself, it's rare you find a writer who's just into books. Most writers are interested in art and visual culture and film and music. And a lot of those things feed into the books, as they did in *Constellations.*

HW: What was it like working with characters?

SG: Oh, really good. You get to have a lot of fun with that. I love Nell, my character. She's an artist, and she's very complicated and independent and doesn't really want much from anything or anybody. She just wants to make her art and have people leave her alone. And then as the book goes on, people keep coming into her life and she doesn't get left alone. With the group, the Inions, they're all from different places and they're all very different people. Writing non-fiction comes from your own life, so you know all the stuff already; as in, you know what art you like, you know what terrible experience you had in the hospital, you know about writing about your family members. But with fiction, you can literally decide, *I can do anything*. And I loved that. Dialogue is difficult. It's something you don't really do in the essay, so that was quite a new thing, learning how people speak.

HW: You did a lot of music journalism in your early years. I'm interested in the idea of music journalists going on to write very interesting long-form work, and how it can be a good training ground. Perhaps part of it is developing an ability to write about things that are intangible, putting colour on things you can't actually see.

SG: Those early days of trying to write about music – it's the old phrase of 'dancing about architecture', because it is difficult to describe, but also, like book criticism, it's quite subjective. Trying to use colours and synonyms and metaphors to describe music is tricky. You're thinking about the words but you're also thinking about the shape of the piece. I remember that I decided not to do print journalism any more because it just felt like all the energy I had for words was going on that. When I was starting to write a bit more, I just thought, *I can talk about books on the radio or the telly, or I can interview people in front of an audience, but I can't do the print stuff anymore.* I do occasionally now, but it tends to be people will ask me because they think I might be interested in the book or it corresponds with my own work in some ways. Also, all writing for me is a piece of writing. It wouldn't just be a case of dashing it off or writing it in a night. I can remember you'd have to go to gigs years ago and review them in two hours so it'd be in the paper the next day. Whether it's a review you get 150 quid for or it's something that's going to be in your book, I still take the same time and care and attention; probably too long, in some cases. If somebody spent years and years writing a book, the least you can do is give it your full time and attention when it comes to critique. Lots of people did that for *Constellations*, including you – I was very grateful for your very insightful review of *Constellations* – and that's a huge gift for a writer, not just because somebody likes it, but because they engage with what you try to do and you learn things about your own work, which I've found one of the most fascinating processes of the whole thing.

HW: Did that happen often with *Constellations*?

SG: Several times. You might remember the essay 'Second Mother'. It's very much about my godmother and the impact she had on me and my brothers, and also the opportunities that certain women from working-class areas didn't have, especially ones who didn't get married. But one thing that kept happening when I did the events was a lot of women came up to me and just said, 'I don't have children,' either 'I couldn't have children' or 'I didn't want to have children', and 'I'm the Auntie Terry.' Lots of people said, 'Women like me are not represented in the culture.' You know, the beloved aunt who does all this, who's like the second mam but doesn't have a place in that nuclear family. And I found that hugely touching. People will transpose their own experience, even if it's not the same as your own. Again, I had a lot of that with people who are ill and sick. I did an event in Cambridge, a literary festival, and there was a woman sitting in the audience in the front row and she was nodding along to everything I said, and she looked very emotional. I thought she was going to ask a question at the end and she didn't, but there was a signing after and I kept seeing her at the back of the queue. Every time she would get near, she'd go to the back of the queue, and I thought, *OK, what's this going to be about?* And she came up and said: 'I was born in a mother-and-baby home in Ireland and it's dominated my life massively, and lots of things you're talking about in your book are really relevant to me. I also have cancer and I'm terminally ill, and I think a lot of that has to do with the pain and the trauma and things that have gone through my life.' She was very emotional and I was very emotional. So you don't know the impact it's going to have. The essay is an act of interrogation, trying to figure out how we feel about a subject by writing about it and engaging with it. And if other people get something from that, whether that's emotional or they learn about an artist or it makes them feel better about their illness or whatever it is, that's an utter bonus and not something I could have foreseen. It was a really humbling thing.

HW: There are things from your essay-writing workshop that I still draw on every day at the desk. Did you find that you could bring a lot of those tools with you into fiction or was it a very different apparatus?

SG: Lots of things are the same, like just showing up, sitting down, plugging in the laptop, even on the days you're like, *I don't want to do this. I'm tired. I've got to do that other work instead of writing this thing that'll probably be rubbish anyway, and I've got to pick people up in the school at this time.* Most days are like that. Most days are not good days in writing. I recently wrote a piece for Jami Attenberg's #1000wordsofsummer about those most dispiriting days when you are trying to write something and you're noticing the clock ticking and ticking and you're just going, *Oh, God, this was the day. I've got other things on, and this was the day to write.* And you get more and more frustrated and you're tempted to just go, *I'll just do the shopping or clean up or whatever.* But you go, *No, I can't let this day pass. I have to do something.* And I wrote about just not giving up and going until the end of the working day and seeing what comes up. And sometimes, weirdly, at five o'clock, when I really think there's nothing going to happen, something happens.

HW: I subscribe to that newsletter. I'm not saying I do 1,000 words a day, but I find there's usually some little nugget of encouragement, even just a sentence, that I can take away.

SG: That's the thing. In terms of your question, what I did try and bring to fiction is that even on the days that you don't get much done, just get a paragraph down. The other thing I found is if I think the thing I'm working on, the place in the book that I am, isn't going well but I know I've got to do something further on, I'll often go off and do that, just to keep the wheels turning because it can be really paralysing to get stuck on something, and then you get frustrated and start to hate that bit of the book. So I wrote it kind of horizontally, which I don't think I will do ever again. I will start at the start and try and go towards the end. But it was all I could do at the time because I wasn't getting that staring-out-the-window time that's really crucial.

HW: Did *Constellations* change your life?

SG: Oh, yeah. For sure. It changed my career and made it viable to try and attempt to write full time. Well, I say full time – I'm not a full-time writer. I never will be because I just think the books industry has changed. A handful of writers are full time but it's just not an economic possibility for most of us. But that's not why we write. We write because we have to. I don't feel myself if I haven't written for a few days. It made me now go, *I've done it once. I have to keep doing it.* I can never go back to those days where I can bunk off and not do it or not maintain the routine or not see something through to the end, which I did before I was a published writer. It's easy to ditch things. It's easy to bail. It's not so easy when you've met a load of people who are like, 'What's your next book about? Are you working on something else?', and that you've found readers, which still always amazes me.

HW: Do you worry about being a writer during a cost-of-living crisis?

SG: Yeah, of course. Like all writers I know, we're doing things we don't necessarily want to do. While being grateful for the work, all of us would like to be writing more than doing things that take up time that don't pay an awful lot of money. That might involve travel that takes you away from your family and your writing. At the same time, I'm always happy to be asked to do things like that. I do want to say at this point I've been the recipient of money from the Arts Council in the past and I'd still be trying to write *Constellations* if I hadn't got a bursary at the time. While there'll always be people who complain there's not enough money or where the money goes or what's happening, I can't stress enough how important those bursaries are. I talk to other writers from the UK who have nothing like the structures that we have. But I do worry, especially with everything just costing so much more. There's the argument of, like, I'm sitting in a room writing something that may or may not end up in a book, so is that a day wasted? I could have done some freelance work and that is money that will go into the bank when I have people to support. There's always that conflict. I think sometimes there's a lot of misconceptions about income and writers. There was a Society of Authors piece where it's something like seven grand a year they reckon most writers earn.

HW: How do you respond to being a parent during the climate emergency?

SG: We're a mostly vegetarian house, and try to be better about consumption, sustainability. It's just little gestures because it feels really overwhelming when you look at anything that's going on and you see the people who don't recycle or have three cars in their driveway. You can't judge other people for the decisions they have to make in their life, but I can only try and make these small incremental ones in my own life and encourage my children. But, yeah, it's extremely, extremely grim, the state that we're in. And it seems that no matter how long it's been said and how vociferously the argument is being made by people who know about this stuff, climatologists or scientists, it still feels like a lot of people are not listening, people in power, people who can do things, who can change things.

HW: Do you believe in civil disobedience, as we're seeing from Just Stop Oil?

SG: I absolutely believe in civil disobedience. Well, it depends – there's degrees of variances. I'm not necessarily down with looting or violence. But, at the same time, there are things that need to be done sometimes to make change. If you look at America and civil rights, sometimes it's absolutely the only way to be heard. Maybe not quite in the vein of civil disobedience, but when you look at Repeal, the marches got bigger and a younger generation joined the conversation, and that felt very important to me. And then that horrific, galvanising moment of Savita Halappanavar dying, when a lot of people just went, 'That has to be it.' While there wasn't disobedience, it was definitely speaking up and saying things. And because we're on the subject of writing, personal testimony was a huge factor in getting both Repeal and Marriage Equality over the line. I know some people who have not been the same since having spoken out on these subjects. Their lives derailed a little bit and they paid a very high price for telling a personal story. When I do workshops with people, I often talk about this, that if you're going to write an essay about something that's very big in your life, especially if it involves other people, you have to be prepared to stand over it, because it might not go the way you necessarily want to go. My mother was very involved in left politics and was always at meetings and going to marches, so I was always quite engaged from when I was young. I really admire a lot of the work that's gone on with people who are turning up at evictions and are prepared to put their own bodies on the line for those being thrown out, often with the gardaí overseeing the whole thing. We're in the middle of a lot of different crises, not just in the world but in Ireland, but if you don't do anything, if you don't say anything and you aren't active about it, things aren't going to change. And then the people who are above all of that, whether that's government or other authorities, will just take that as complicity and maybe even try and push things further. So, yeah, it's very important to speak up, to be active, by whatever means you want to do. I canvassed a lot during those campaigns. I got a lot of 'no's at first, but then you start to talk to people and they listen and it can turn things around. That's something you can't necessarily do with the internet or online, that one to one, that humanity, that encouragement of empathy. People ask me what *Constellations* is about, and I always said it was a book about empathy.

HW: Why do you think the essay is having a moment in this country in particular?

SG: It's all linked into our social, political and cultural history, a culture of being told to be quiet, being told to shut up. And I don't just mean women. A fear of authority. A fear of the Church. The idea of living in small towns and that if somebody knew something terrible about you, that your family wasn't perfect, that you had a drinking problem, that you'd had an abortion, any of these things. The unwritable, the unsayable. It's having a moment because, in Ireland, we've changed more in the last ten years than the last sixty or seventy, and out of that social and cultural change people have found their voices and people have things they want to say. Myself and Emilie Pine did a lot of events together around that time. She's an incredible writer and a lovely person, and we said a lot at the time that ten years before that I'm not sure books like ours would have been published. There was a whole breaking down of silences, where people wanted to hear these voices and a lot of that was aligned to those referenda as well, people starting to speak and talk about things that happened that felt singular and personal, but then when you tell a story like that, it ends up becoming something much bigger. Look at all the silencing around abuse. People didn't talk about the things that were terrible, and often in essays people want to write about those things that are not necessarily joyful or funny. Of course, there are many exceptions – Samantha Irby, Patrick Freyne, people like that – but mostly people are grappling with something that's difficult, that they want to figure out. And it's been interesting to see not everybody's writing straightforward, linear stuff. There's been a lot of messing around with the form, which is exciting to see. One of the best students in the MA class I had in UCD, Jayne A. Quan, published a collection last year with Skein Press [*All this happened, more or less*], which was just incredible and inventive and moving and sad, but also funny as well.

HW: You spoke before about the importance of being published in journals very early in your career, and how it gave you self-belief when you really needed it. We seem to have more titles than ever in Ireland now.

SG: Absolutely. I literally don't think I'd be a writer without the existence of that kind of infrastructure. The idea of *I'm writing a book* was just not something I ever said to myself. It was too daunting. It was too much of a time commitment. It felt like a thing that other people did and not me. But essays are a very compact, bendy, malleable form. You can literally do anything with them. For me, there are less rules within them than short stories. It could be a page; it could be fifteen pages. There are essays that look like novellas and there are ones like, you know, Lydia Davis, that are a paragraph. I didn't send to any of the journals really, but I loved the idea of *Banshee*, this new feminist journal, because this piece ['Hair'] was about hair and the body and religion and the Church and preconceptions of what hair means in culture, in sexuality and identity, where it was in art and politics, head shavings in the War of Independence. It just seemed like the right place to send it. I didn't for a moment assume it would be published, which it was. After that, two pieces got published in *Granta*, and that changed everything. The first one, 'Blue Hills and Chalk Bones', got a huge response that I didn't expect. And at that point, Peter Straus, who is my agent, said to me, 'Have you got a book?' And I literally didn't. I just had these essays. The second *Granta* one ['Second Mother'] hadn't been published at that point. And he just said, 'I'd really like to take you on to write a book.' He didn't hassle me because he knew I was nervous and had other commitments. He just said come back to me when you think you've got a book. And that's what I did. So those journals were a lifeline. And it's funny. I never sent any work to the *Stinging Fly* or the *Dublin Review*. At the time, Brendan [Barrington] was always publishing non-fiction. The *Stinging Fly*, more so now, but for a long time it didn't publish much non-fiction. But the fact that we now have *Tolka*, this publication that acknowledges the level, the talent and the volume of non-fiction, and that it's being taken seriously . . . In a way, for a long time people didn't know what an essay was or were confused about the form, what it could do, that maybe people were writing essays because it was easier to write from your own life – it's not – than writing a piece of made-up fiction. Whether it's a workshop at a festival or in UCD, where I had been writer-in-residence, lots of the people I teach don't have agents or book deals. You have to start somewhere and the idea of writing a whole book is quite daunting. But accumulating a body of work and sending them out, one by one, to various places and building a little CV in different publications, that's the kind of stuff that helps people get agents. You're a writer whether you send the work out or not, but most writers are not writing to put it in the drawer. They're writing to find readers and the easiest way to find readers is to put the work out in the world, and the first and most valuable platform I can think of is those journals.

Soft Ground

SHANNAN MANN

I have been thinking about breasts lately. I feel my own breasts without touching them. I feel them as one feels the prickly edge of a tag on a new dress. I have seen enough advertisements, movies and magazines to know what kind of breasts are considered conventionally perfect. I've never had anything close to that. I contemplate the jealousy in my body. I hold the ebb and flow of emotions as one sloshes water inside their mouth before spitting. I do not have perfect breasts. I hold this thought before me. I find it neither intrusive nor hurtful, neither silly nor wasteful. This is soft ground for deeper excavation.

I cannot remember how my breasts looked as a teenager. I no longer have the nudes I sent to one or two boys. Perhaps they still have them. I do remember, though, that they were smaller than I'd have liked them to be. There is nothing extraordinary about a girl wanting a bigger, bouncier pair. I cannot even completely remember my breasts before pregnancy; however, this is something I do recall.

Towards the second week of November 2019, as I was cleaning the bathroom, I felt rings of blades around my nipples. I lifted my shirt and stared in curious horror at the reflection that greeted me. Overnight, my breasts had transformed. Imagine if this happened to a different body part – waking up to a boneless arm or with eyebrows morphed into a squirrel's tail. I moved closer to the mirror and noticed the areolae. Their circumference had at least tripled and the color had changed from hazelnut to the kind of brown one is inclined to label black. The milk-duct orifices glistened with an eroded redness. They resembled kumkum, coarse sandstone, crushed maple leaves in October.

I suspected I was pregnant. The test I took the morning after confirmed that. But the changes in my body stopped a few weeks later. My quietly expanding breasts paused their takeover of my chest and the redness in the areolae roughened back into the familiar hazelnut. I remember blood – a mix of body and baby – on the bathroom floor of a restaurant. I reached down in between my legs, as if this delicate act of placing palm over vulva could keep the microscopic heartbeat inside alive.

We ended up in the ER around four in the morning. I was directed to a nook behind a white curtain where I lay down on a white bed. They ran some tests and confirmed the miscarriage. A few doctors came in and said a few things. I remember asking if they were sure. And then the sweet, sweaty smell of nitrous oxide coated my teeth and throat and billowed into my lungs. Everything was louder but far away. There was metal and a finger inside me. I was told to go home and rest. At home I peed and did not glance at the reddened toilet bowl. I looked in the mirror, lifted my shirt, and touched my breasts. I hated how normal they felt, how still and lifeless.

Many months later, when Ana was conceived, I waited to feel the same changes. They did not come as they had with the first pregnancy. And Ana stayed, she did not leave. My breasts did hurt, though. More so when morning sickness began. They grew also, and so did the rest of me. So fast. Ana was like a little sun inside my womb, enforcing her light over the shadow of my body. I gained far more weight than allocated to her, the placenta and the amniotic fluid. I was always hungry and I was always throwing up and I was always afraid of losing another baby.

Some women's nipples leak in pregnancy. Mine did not. Not everyone's do. By the third trimester, my breasts were more nipple than breast. The day my water broke I wiped a bud of translucent liquid from the left areola. The midwife asked me to wear a maternity pad and try to sleep – we'd meet in the birthing suite in the morning. But the pad soon filled up with meconium and blood and we were once again rushing to emergency. The contractions grew at breakneck speed. Far from the natural delivery I'd imagined, I ended up strapped to a bed with monitors beeping around me. I couldn't move. I finally begged for an epidural after fourteen hours of labour, but it was Christmas Eve and there was minimal staff and an overabundance of birthing women. The doctors couldn't agree on how pressing my condition was. One felt the pitocin should be upped to expedite a vaginal delivery. Another felt I needed to be rushed to an emergency caesarean. It was only when Ana's heartrate became frighteningly high that I was prepped for the operation. The epidural arrived. I was relieved I'd hold my baby soon. About an hour later, cut open and bleeding out, I was screaming and fading in and out of consciousness while Ana was being resuscitated by a team of twenty medical professionals. She suffered an extreme case of meconium aspiration, pneumonia, sepsis and pulmonary hypertension. I'd developed a freak intrauterine infection and, also, had sepsis. I'd lost far too much blood in the C-section. I was lucky, my midwife told me later. But for the first six days of Ana's ventilated life, I didn't feel lucky at all. It wasn't until the day after New Year's that I knew she'd live.

The first night, I was alone in a hospital room and she was many miles away in another hospital better equipped to take care of her. A nurse came into my room and said she could squeeze and stimulate my breasts so the milk flow would begin. Colostrum, she explained, was liquid gold, and this was something I could do for my baby even from here – give her this essential irreplaceable food, nature's talisman against any bacterial evil eye. Ana was getting morphine instead.

The nurse pushed down into my heart, breastbone, to the side toward my armpits, in between cleavage (although I did not have much of a cleavage because by now the breasts were falling to the sides rather than resting in the middle as they had done before pregnancy) and then finally C-cupped her hands, squeezed out and down towards the nipple and pressed out the tiniest flower-bud drops of yellow-blue colostrum. She tilted my nipple into a syringe and let the drops collect inside. We did this for twenty minutes every two hours, to emulate what a baby would do. The pain was excruciating. My entire body hardened like a corpse with rigor mortis each time she drew out milk. There were no motherly hormones acquired from nursing a newborn, from tender lips closing around your breast and teasing out a slow flow of nourishment. Only cold hands, quiet tears, empty breasts. And they *were* empty. My milk did not come in properly for two weeks. That, too, required medication, herbs and copious amounts of oats, paneer and pumpkin. Still the milk was not enough.

The next morning I was transferred to the Wellington Hospital, where Ana was being treated in the NICU. I was in a wheelchair. Walking felt like stepping out of a frozen lake. A lactation consultant gave me a breast pump and told me to sit next to my baby and 'dry pump' for twenty minutes every two hours to trigger my breasts to produce milk. Ana was in her little bed in stimulated sleep. I was awake in mine, stimulating milk.

Every now and again a nurse would come, touch my breasts, squeeze them like large lemons, flesh out drops of milk, sometimes a spray of white into a syringe and Ana's father would take those syringes to her in her little cold bed of morphine sleep.

I pumped every two hours for thirty minutes to an hour. Day and night for several weeks. Time was measured in milliliters of milk. Often, the pump caused so much pain that I'd bite the insides of my cheeks and force my hands over the pump cups, pressing down even though every impulse in my body wanted to remove them, to throw them away. When we were shifted to Hutt Hospital (after Ana started getting better), I pumped in the pumping room. All the mothers who came there would fill up bottles of milk in what seemed like minutes and I'd sit there for an hour, only ever getting to half the bottle beneath each breast.

I became more obsessed with my breasts than a teenager. I detested them for their utter uselessness. I was absorbed in searching for a cure. I was told that my birth trauma (just the physical trauma itself, not even touching on the emotional) likely contributed to a low supply, and then the stress pushed it further. But I thought surely there must be more, surely it cannot just be that, surely my breasts have a structural problem, an inner emptiness that does not allow the fullness of milk. I felt deformed and numb. Each drop of white was a drop of blood. My nipples often bled from the pump. And my breasts continued to loosen, sag, soften, like those Ziplock bags they give you in pet stores with a little bit of water and your goldfish fluttering its tiny fins, aching for its fishbowl because it does not know an ocean.

When I stopped breastfeeding (or *depressed feeding* as I called it), I lost about twelve kilograms in three weeks because I lost my appetite. I lost more weight quite rapidly over the next several months. The loss of appetite brought on a desire to fast and the fasting fostered more loss of appetite. One thing I rarely did was look at myself in the mirror. I could not stand to see my naked reflection. I'd step out of the shower and twirl a towel around me (Ana was a good excuse for the quickness of this motion), hiding myself away from myself. I was afraid and embarrassed. I wished some magic herb existed. I wished for a time machine to have my before-baby body again, or better yet to have my teenage body again. Even though I'd always had small breasts then, at least they were relatively normal. Now, everything was overtaken by gravity in the way an abandoned town is overtaken by wildlife.

I touch my breasts – too soft, elastic and the right too much to the right, the left too much to the left, the gap in the middle far too wide when I lie down, and the nipples curving up. I touch my stomach with its textured ripples, waterbed motion, pillowy surface, and the scar between belly and vulva. I touch my inner thighs, examine my arms and shrug my shoulders. For much of my adult life I ascribed to the philosophy that we are not our bodies. I still believe that. At the same time, I am aware there are so many beautiful bodies. Bodies with beautiful breasts, and a few even with perfect breasts. I look at my sleeping daughter and think how one day she too will have an opinion about perfection.

Ana nuzzles closer to me. Perhaps she can still smell the drying milk inside my sagging breasts. The breast pump now sits in a box of baby things to be donated, along with the nursing bra and breast pads I never needed. Sometimes I'm walking on the street with Ana kangarooed inside a wrap and I catch myself checking out other women's breasts. Envy, as a favourite poet of mine writes, is the only sin that is no fun for the sinner. I hope I'll reach a space where I'll see more of the beauty in this new love for gravity my body has acquired, the kintsugi map of stretchmarks shimmering down my armpits, loping under my waist, kissing the edge of my nipples. And little Anasuya resting her lavender-blossom head upon me – perfectly content with the marshmallow softness of my limp, hollow breasts.

Silent Hills

CONOR DAWSON

'At first you didn't know me.'
Cynthia Huntington, 'Ghost'

only up the road

Long after midnight I wheel my bicycle uphill, guided by a blinking torch through a darkness that shifts between extremes. From an open, lunar dark to the closed form of a long tunnel. Something shifts in me, too; I hear breathing that is not entirely my own. *It's only up the road*, I say to myself and no one. The slope rises and leafless trees force the backroad to the width of a lane. My torch dies in cold, wet fingers, and I fear I'm not alone.

Back in the granny flat, I shrug myself free of the hi-vis and peel off my dripping rain jacket. Rubbery skin clenches bone. Before I know what I'm doing, my laptop is open on the coffee table and I have to stop myself from watching another playthrough. Instead, I read the script of a game I've never played. Confronted with this line, I pause: 'The only me is me. Are you sure the only you is you?' The curtains are half-pulled, half-parted over a strip of light-stained glass. To see past would be to see the driveway dip towards the backroad where darkness inhabits the eye and mind, where *me* and *you* might be multiple. My eyes dilate to let out the dark: the colour of my laptop screen on standby might be the exact shade of blackout before a respawn.

P. T.

Some years earlier, summer found me between jobs and cities, back home where my brother Shane said he had something to show me on his PS4. As we entered the living room, our dad passed us on his way out. Stood at the doorway, he savoured a puff off his vape like it was smoke from an heirloom cigar. In his eyes there was the look of pale stone. Carved and hardened since my childhood when he had to leave his childhood home. At our backs the door closed, and I could taste peppermint in the spot where words form.

The loading screen displayed a photographic still of a wooded field: the greens withered to yellow in patches, tree limbs blackened by a silvery sky; to the side, a blocky stump with the letters P. T. overlaid in Tipp-Ex white. A path curved through the grass, vanishing behind thicket. The type of place where you might find a gang of teenagers necking cans. Hidden behind some narrow backroad. Then the screen blacked out, and I could hear fear as resonance, as echo, when a door pulled itself open.

For the next hour I watched Shane explore the dark hallway of a suburban home in the playable teaser for *Silent Hills*, the abandoned collaboration between game designer Hideo Kojima and film director Guillermo del Toro. Much like the half-seen woman in white who haunts the hallway, this teaser now hovers between presence and absence, between life and death. A fragment from an unrealised whole, removed from PlayStation's online store in response to the project's sudden dissolution. While the downloaded teaser would eventually increase the value of Shane's PlayStation enough for him to consider selling it, its shock value far exceeded anything an online auction might rake in. So, the console stayed tucked under the television stand in our parents' living room.

I sat in silence, spooked by the atmospherics, and unnerved by the memories of murder that slowly bled down the walls of the home. 'Haunting is about a staining of place with particularly intense moments of time,' writes Mark Fisher in *Ghosts of My Life*. In the game, these moments in time return through a series of increasingly cryptic puzzles, while the woman in white stalks you in the hallway, at the edge of torchlight, waiting. By the bathroom, the lights go out; unseen, she makes a noise between breathing and choking. Anticipating a jump scare, Shane turned. A bright shape in tight first person. Strobe-lit dark, then a corpse-white face in close-up. The torch drops to the floor, spotlighting the wall while you bleed out.

Lying on the floor, the character respawns. A hand presses against concrete, the unzipped sleeve of a leather jacket briefly visible. Shane offered me the controller, but I waved him off. Smiling, he stared into the screen. The door was just ahead, a few steps further through the dark where fear lingered, resonant, an echo of an older fear.

a door opens

In his study of the *Silent Hill* series, Bernard Perron writes that 'the typical starting point for any discussion about *Silent Hill* is a comparison to *Resident Evil*'. My first memories of these survival horror games bear out Perron's assertion. In my mind, the two games are two rooms in a hyperreal haunted house, separated by a long dark hallway. To reach *Silent Hill*, I had to first pass through the great hall of *Resident Evil*, and then through the long dark of a feeling older than words.

The original *Resident Evil* was first released for the PlayStation in 1996, on the day of my seventh birthday. At some point that year, I sat on the carpet in my cousin's bedroom, knees tucked to my chest, staring into a boxy television. The stark white of the initial load-up screen faded to black. Otherworldly sounds, synths that played icy tones. My cousin warned me that the game was scary, and I felt alone in that room. I wasn't sure what 'resident' or 'evil' meant, but I knew well that this game wasn't like the others I had played before, that I was being allowed a glimpse into a shadowy place levels beyond the two-dimensional blue skies and rollercoaster hills of *Sonic the Hedgehog*.

I remember bits of the opening sequence to *Resident Evil*, scenes from a black-and-white B movie. Metallic curves of grass, mist thicker than smoke. Nameless things lurking at the edge of vision and imagination. The B movie intro cut to a load-up screen, to our fuzzy reflections trapped behind glass. Out of that darkness, three blocky figures step into an echoey, pixelated manor. White tiles squared off along a red carpet that climbs a divided staircase. As in an episode of *Scooby-Doo*, the three figures decide, foolishly enough, to split up; the screen blacks out, and a first-person camera guides you through a set of torchlit double doors opening into darkness, to clockwork sounds, a steady tapping that chiselled silence.

Three years later, I watched on as other doors opened into darkness. I can't remember the opening sequence to *Silent Hill*, if it had one at all, but I remember how the camera tracked the character through an expanse of snowy haze, the empty streets of the town misted to the texture of dreams.

Even with my cousin just behind me, I felt alone, focused on the spectral world of the screen. At this stage I had the words to describe this immersive feeling. I was afraid, and this was fear, to see things flicker in and out of being at the glitchy edge of torchlight. To see what else might emerge from the night.

night

Of its many subtler effects, the pandemic manages to invert a line from Philip Larkin, so that life is first fear, and then boredom. In year zero of this new fear, I find myself stranded in a granny flat at the edge of a small coastal town of briny winds and endless backroads. During the day the sky hardens from shale grey to granite, until evening shades the land Nordic and dark. On a walk down grassy backroads, the flightpaths of bats arc close overhead; in the time it takes me to blink, the bats flit through the jagged reach of gothic trees.

I make a deal with a man my father's age in a garage whose grip is calloused and oily. In the front of the garage the air is pure turpentine, his eyes tundra blue. He agrees to sell me his last second-hand bicycle, even if I am a blow-in. 'The roads are bad,' he says. 'The best struggle.' Though the cyclists stayed away during the summer just gone. He reckons winter will be the same, and as the short days grow shorter, he'll turn out to be right.

When he asks what brought me out here, I don't tell him that I don't really know. I mention something about the digital hub and the promise of a reliable internet connection. In a jokey tone, he asks what good is high-speed internet when the roads are so slow. 'It's like cycling on sand,' he says. He wipes an oily hand off his jeans. As soon as he turns, I do the same, wiping my palm off my tracksuit pants.

He takes me round the back to the bicycle, where he pinches the tyres to check the air pressure. From here the sea is slate-still, the mountains brownish fog in the distance. When he tries to get me to talk football, I can hear months of solitude in the silence between words. After the first lockdown small talk doesn't come as easily as it used to. When I hand over a fifty euro note, he throws in a helmet and a small bicycle pump.

That day I don't cross paths with another person. With eight years abroad behind me in cities with strange languages that make little to no sense, I imagine that I will cope with the silence quite well.

After midnight I wake up in the granny flat to strap a torch to my helmet. In the black glass of the front door my hi-vis gives me the look of some crackpot guard on a one-man nightshift. I hype myself up for the cycle to the other side of town. There is a novelty to this, an absurdity that edges on excitement. Outside, the cold is something thrown over me, watery in its thickness. Nervously I fasten the bicycle pump to the frame.

On the backroad, the dark is not one colour, not one shade of black. Here, the night is its own spectrum, so that the smoke-thick air disperses into dark mists, and the mists into sepia-tinted tarmac at the town's edge after the cold rush downhill. Past the vivid white statue of the Virgin Mary in the town square, other darks open onto empty roads where the night hangs depthless: the twenty-five-kilometre journey to the next town over cuts through a vast, nocturnal terrain, all sense of distance eclipsed despite the road signs. As for the feel of the road, the man in the garage was right. The last stretch is hard going and in bad need of resurfacing. I attribute the small miracle of my arrival at the digital hub to the statue.

The carpark might be a study in the variant of the eerie that Mark Fisher called 'a failure of presence'. There is *nothing* where there should be *something*. At the back where the tarmac gives way to waste ground and long grass, there's a disused tractor. A lone remnant of presence before the absence set in.

Inside, this failure of presence sustains itself along the empty unlit hallway. The lights hesitate between on and off. I take an office to myself with windows that face onto the road. It's early morning in Shanghai, where most of the impossibly chirpy students who take these extra classes live. The thought of the cycle uphill in the dark plays on my imagination throughout. Soon enough it starts to feel like I'm speaking to myself with the sole intention of taking my mind off the return journey.

By the time I finish teaching for the night, I'm childish and giddy with fear. At the door to the carpark, I zip up my rain jacket and shimmy into my hi-vis. The glass screen stained with fluorescence, with my own insomniac pallor. In the darkness beyond, an image from an arthouse horror film I flicked onto by chance when I was too young to be watching such things returns to stare me down. Along a barren stretch of road, a pale woman in a white dress hobbles towards streetlight in a long take. Her eye shadow charcoal-heavy, like Jane in *The Cabinet of Dr Caligari*. In the film she is alone, though she speaks to herself. In Italian or French. I'm not sure why this image suddenly comes to me, though the visual recall feels pristine, if not the content of her monologue.

Briny rain spatters against glass, and then against my face as I lock up. I get the sense that the animate darkness beyond is intent on showing me other images drowned in time. I cycle back as quickly as I can, skirting past the statue of the Virgin Mary, eyes averted. On a later cycle, breathless on the slope of the backroad, my bicycle pump will plummet through the void, rolling downhill. Fearing another apparition of the pale woman, I will not think to stop.

alone

Perron goes on to note that 'to be true to the genre, survival horror games should be played at night when you are "alone in the dark", and even better, when everyone else is asleep'. This is for a simple enough reason, so that 'the solitary experience of the character mirrors the player's experience'.

There is fear in this loneliness, but also in observing someone else's loneliness. On a night off from classes, I try to track down the horror film with the pale woman online. My search terms are vague at first, and then increasingly frantic. I end up on YouTube watching a playthrough of *Silent Hills*. As in my earliest memories of the series, I sit in a trance as someone else leads the way.

In darkness, you begin again. A pair of conjoined cockroaches creep across concrete. A door opens, a hi-def reimagining of much older doors. You enter the hallway of a dimly lit suburban home. Framed photographs decorate the walls. The sound of your steps exaggerated by hardwood flooring as you round the corner. Cigarettes stubbed out on a tabletop. Empty beer cans, a teddy bear ragdolled to the floor. Beyond the corner, a staticky radio plays. 'We regret to report the murder of the wife and her two children by their husband and father,' says a voice in bassy monotone. Right next to the radio, a black-and-white photograph of a happy couple on their wedding day.

At the end of the hallway, beer cans and bottles line a second door, locked for now. The radio report further details the death of the family, noting that the wife was pregnant at the time of the murder, and that the father lured his six-year-old daughter out of her hiding place in the bathroom by telling her that 'it was just *a game*'. This moment of self-reflexive gallows humour is drowned out by the rest of the report. The police eventually found the father, listening to the radio in his car, a detail that creates a parallel between you and the perpetrator.

Before the radio cuts out, the reporter notes that this crime restaged older crimes. Two other murders were committed by fathers in similar circumstances in recent years. You are left listening to the sound of white noise. The second door opens. You descend a few steps down a darkened stairway into a concrete cellar where you push open the door to another room, only to find yourself back at the start of the dimly lit hallway.

Years after watching Shane play the game for the first time, I realise that the player has just passed through an impossible space. The L-shaped hallway seems to loop back on itself, as if drawn up by MC Escher. Despite this perfect circularity, the stairs marks a slow progression downward: with each recurring entrance, you descend deeper into a space derealised by fantasies of guilt.

On the second loop a third door bangs violently, as if someone is trapped inside. An echo of the earlier radio report informs us that the daughter hid in the bathroom as the father murdered her mother and brother. On the next loop, the door at the end of the hallway slams shut, while another door opens into the bathroom. When the woman appears in a shade of psychotropic white, I stop the playthrough and abandon my search for the nameless woman from the film.

the woman in white

The virus spreads through early winter, and in the local supermarket the space between customers grows. This town of five hundred might have an average age of about sixty. The nearest hospital is an hour down cruel roads glazed with neglect. In time the entire island will rift into town-sized archipelagos like this.

On the days I don't bother with the supermarket, I see no one, and the night cycles continue in the dark. I soon find that I don't enjoy the solitude of the graveyard shift in the digital hub. Somehow, the students remain chirpy, even as I drone on about how *this* means *that*, and how *that* means *this*. I make gestures with my hands that they probably can't see. I try not to think of the woman in white on the way back each night, but at the same narrow point where the darkness deepens and the slope of the backroad rises, I feel her breathe alongside me. Speed blurs form, so that on a given night she might resemble the statue of the Virgin Mary in flashback, or the orb of my torch on cottage windows. A marble cailleach, or a revenant *yūrei* from a J-horror film like *The Ring*.

Here, in this town of briny rains and endless backroads, Japanese ghost women might seem hopelessly out of place. But unlike their American counterparts, J-horror 'films are as infused with sadness as horror', as Charles Derry notes in his history of the horror film. This mood is familiar to smalltown coastal Ireland. Consider this passage from Mike McCormack's novel, *Notes from a Coma*: 'What no tourist bumf will tell you is that this inlet is suffused with an atmosphere of ineffable sadness. Partly a trick of the light.' There is horror here, too, under skies harder than granite; this is 'the type of light wherein ghosts go their rounds at all hours of the day', to say nothing of the night.

Rain scented by the sea and hailstone cold scatters across the carpark, battering the bonnet and the windshield of the tractor. I brace myself and lock up quickly. I roll my bicycle out from the pebble-dashed wall and the back tyre sags. When I sit on top of the saddle, I can feel the rim scrape along the tarmac. I hop off and push the bicycle ahead of me. By the time I make it into town, the rain eases so that I can see the statue with rinsed, beatified clarity. Past the empty pubs and shuttered chipper, I force myself to walk towards the football pitch where the road forks towards the backroad.

The rain stops. The night closes in; the tunnel of my torch's throw distance shortens. There is something ancient out here, something eternal. Neither alive nor dead, like the stars whose light is yet to reach this frozen boreen. Older than the first words that shaped flesh and thought into what we would become. I feel the slope gain, but nothing moves. In this darkness slowed to stillness, there is no distinction between the world and what I might think of it. The white cone of light summons memories of things I still don't understand, free-floating and of the land itself. Some way on, the darkness deepens; the slope spikes, and my torch gives in, blinking, then blind. I walk on through total dark. My runners squeak on wet grass and I wait for the woman in white to emerge from a lightless nook at the back of my eyes. For all the time I've spent watching out for her, in the end I sense that she's been watching me a lot longer.

the only true madness

You knock against the bathroom door, trapped inside the scene of the crime. A perfect circle of torchlight haloes the darkness. Cockroaches crawl across blood-stained tiles. The torch lamps a foetus-like creature in the sink, a mewling thing torn from David Lynch's *Eraserhead*. You face the mirror, torch raised, but scratch marks and black streaks stain the reflection from sight.

Outside the bathroom, the reporter continues his description of the crime. 'After killing his family, the father hung himself with a garden hose they had in the garage.' Layered beneath, a muffled echo: 'The father hung himself with an umbilical cord they had in the garage.' Contradictions that contradict the earlier report of the father's arrest. These memories are not singular, the haunted families are multiple.

The week before Christmas, the town's two pubs open. I meet the dayshift workers of the digital hub at a pre-booked table for pints. It feels strange to talk and the words are slow and unfamiliar at first.

When I head up for my round, I bump into the man from the garage. His eyes retain their shade of tundra blue. 'I hear you're on the night shift down below,' he says. He's a reader himself and I should have told him that I was teaching literature. He quizzes me with a line on the spot. 'The only true madness is loneliness,' he says. 'The monotonous voice in the skull that never stops because never heard.'

'Beckett,' I guess, and he smiles.

It's early when I walk up the backroad, torchlight restored. Before midnight, and long before the deepest darkness is due to settle over the place. The next morning, I will half-remember the line and find a poem by John Montague online. A poem about the mythical cailleach, about 'ancient awe, the terror of a child', about loneliness bruised by age and silence.

In the afternoon I take a walk to clear my head. Though I have lived much farther from home, I feel lost. On the other side of town I wander into the woods. I remember some of that ancient awe, my own childhood terror glimpsed right after my first exposure to survival horror. A manor in the flatlands of the Curragh, where I raced down a long dark hallway, pushing doors that opened onto empty rooms. Behind one door that wouldn't fully open, a gaunt sculptor worked a slab of marble to the shape of bone and woman. He met my eyes with surprise, and I ran away on legs brittle with shock.

Reversing over the gravel driveway, my mum said the manor was once our home. 'She forced your father out,' she said. 'Before your first words.' I was glad to be getting away from the half-formed woman. Away from those eyes crazed by white stone. For that was fear, too, a loneliness I didn't understand. Years later when I came across notes for a story inside one of my mum's schoolbooks, I recognised the manor's gravel driveway. And the married couple, a young family evicted by family, by a woman pale with age. In early summer, the couple closed the door for the last time, locking the sadness and horror that precede words inside.

erasure

Weeks after Christmas, back at my parents' unheatable bungalow, a storm circles towards us. Soon the silence between lightning and thunder shortens, so close streak and strike coincide in white shocks of sound.

When Shane goes to power up his PlayStation days later, he stares in disbelief at the screen. The machine's hard drive wiped by the storm. Shane downloads most of his games again easily enough, *Grand Theft Auto V*, *The Witcher III*, but the *Silent Hills* teaser has vanished.

Now, whenever I stare into black screens, I know the woman in white resides in the dark at the back of my eyes. Where *me* shades into *you*, and we are not alone.

Notes from a Room

RUBY EASTWOOD

1

In the photos on the rental site, my room looked significantly bigger thanks to a fisheye lens and the tactical placement of a long mirror, which has since been removed. If I lie starlike on the bed I can almost touch all four walls. The single bed takes up most of the space and is significantly bigger than the narrow doorway, so that the frame must have been brought in little pieces and assembled carefully inside, like those miniature sailing boats that are built inside bottles.

2

The walls are thin and newly built, set grid-like into the old frame of the building, splitting the space into tiny compartments. At night I can hear doors opening and closing, water rushing down the pipes, distant music, seagulls nesting on the ceiling. From my window I can see the dark line of trees at the edge of the street, the tents under the overpass, the dim shape of office blocks in the distance and the pinpricks of light at the top of cranes.

3

According to you it wasn't so much the size of the room that was the problem, it was its monkish bareness, its anonymity. You arrived one day unexpectedly, hair wet from the rain, a long roll of paper bound tightly with a hairband under your coat. It was a Man Ray: red lips stretched over a wide horizon, dark hills, mottled clouds. You unrolled it and stuck it with chewing gum to the wall.

4

I, being poor, have only twenty euros in overdraft, a cracked phone, an old laptop, the clothes piled up on the floor, red lipstick, a packet of Ibuprofen half-opened on the bedside table, a chipped blue mug, a ballpoint pen, tangled headphones, an empty packet of tobacco, a half pack of filters, a snakeskin handbag, the diaries of Sylvia Plath, and my dreams.

5

I work in a pub where the old men go. I remember one man who ordered drinks, fumbled in his empty wallet, then reached in his back pocket and gave me a curled-up note. When I uncurled it, white powder fell onto the counter and, despite his wrinkled eyes and balding head, the smile he gave me was distinctly boyish.

6

Almost everyone I know is stuck in Dublin as if in a bad dream, desperate to escape yet unable to move. In periods of hope, we work long shifts and save up, thinking of our future freedom. In periods of despair we work long shifts and spend it all, thinking of our imminent alleviation. The notion of escaping hangs over us like a promise. The conversation always follows the same familiar bends, ending at the same place.

'Tired of this.'

'What.'

'Don't you ever get tired of this.'

'Can't hear you. Music's too loud. Speak up.'

'Let's get out of here. Let's go somewhere for a change.'

'Not much else open at this time.'

'No, I mean really get out. Road trip. Fresh air. Only for a few days. Let's leave in the morning. Get back Monday.'

'Got work tomorrow.'

'Sick'ner.'

'Yeah. Buy us a drink, will you.'

'No money.'

'Sick'ner. Have you got the bag.'

'Thought I gave it back to you.'

7

But once, we really did escape. We took a train along the coast and walked past the county limits. The grass flowers were just beginning to bloom by the train tracks behind the metal railings. It was the first day of real sun, and as we walked through fields and clambered over the rocks, we entered a delirious, childish mood. You picked up a stick and peeled off the bark, and swished it in the air as you walked. The seaweed piled up in the sun. Dark, lazy flies crawled into the moisture of our clothes and skin. We put our towels and bags down in a small clearing where the rocks and seaweed gave way to a strip of small white shells. I rolled up the bottoms of my jeans and let the waves wash over my feet, and behind me you took off your clothes and appeared by the water in a leopard-print bikini. When you walked into the sea, your skin was so pale it shone out underwater, green like glass. You came back and lay on your towel next to me, head bent over a book, water dripping from the tips of your hair, making the edges of the pages go curly. That was the first day you kissed me, leaning over sleepily like it was the most natural thing in the world. Later, coming out of the water, I stepped on a fishing hook.

'Stay still,' you said. The heel of my foot was pink and yellow with a bright red gash across. You felt for the edges and brought it out delicately, then examined it with interest.

'You're not squeamish,' I said.

'My dad's a butcher,' you said.

8

The perimeters of my life are marked by three points: my room, the pizzeria, the pub. The furthest I venture outside of this little triangle is to walk through the cobbled streets on the Southside. I peer in to the big windows of Georgian houses lit soft gold, all dark wood and velvet curtains, intricate flowers blooming on the wallpaper. Their colours are romantic: peach, violet, pea green. My desire is sharpened by anger, though it's hard to tell if I'm angry at the rich for living a life I feel is morally reprehensible, or whether my anger is really at myself, for knowing that I will cease to care the moment such a life comes within my reach.

9

You told me one day that you often think that if you just got nice furniture and did the laundry everything would be different. I have a copy of Jean Rhys's *Good Morning, Midnight* that I had meant to give you. 'Suddenly I feel that I must have Room Number 219, with rose-coloured curtains, carpet and bath,' she writes. 'I will exist on a different plane at once if I can get this room, if only for a couple of nights. Who says you can't escape from your fate? I'll escape from mine, into room 219.'

10

When I see nice rooms, it's comforting to think of the flawed lives set within: the wives who spend all day drowsy on prescription pills, moving the furniture and rearranging the flowers, matching the carpets to the wallpaper. The idea that it might be possible to have a beautiful house and a beautiful life is offensive. The rooms might be big, but the walls would surely begin to close in over the years until there is no space to breathe.

11

Louise Bourgeois's housewife paintings show naked women protruding out of tiny houses, their genitals exposed, their heads boxed up. The paintings are like that image in *Alice in Wonderland*, after she drinks the potion and she grows so big that her head is crushed against the ceiling and her limbs hang out of the windows. The difference is that Louise Bourgeois's world is the real world, not dreamland, and there is no antidote that will restore everything to manageable proportions.

12

When we got back to Dublin the sky was darkening. The sudden cold of that spring night took us by surprise, and we walked across the platform with our arms interlinked, huddled together. You had never been to my room. I insisted we go to yours instead, but when we got there your friends were having a party. You had invited them for brunch earlier. They had a way of hanging around. You asked me if you should tell them to go but I said no point, they're here now, and you agreed.

'Who's that?' you asked. There was someone at the far end of the room, seemingly unconscious.

'That's Joe,' came a reply. 'Isn't he hilarious?' Your friend offered me a drink and I said no, I could never catch up, I was too far behind. He said Joe had only arrived an hour before us and he had been completely sober.

13

The first time we broke up I took down the poster, but the chewing gum stains remained on the wall, marking your absence. Over the next few months, the poster was restored and taken down again more times than I care to remember.

14

When you first told me about your sugar daddy I pictured a fairytale for us. I said that with any luck he would die suddenly and leave everything to you. I secretly imagined us living in his house, with bookshelves so enormous they came with little sliding ladders. I pictured you on the back of a white horse, galloping over hills, hair streaming out behind you. We would host lavish dinner parties where I would describe my old room in North Dublin with great irony.

'Remember that ghastly blue carpet!' you would say.

'The frightful smell!' I would reply.

The distinguished company would find this all very amusing. You punctured my illusions. You said he wasn't that old so it was unlikely that he would die anytime soon, though luckily enough he was completely impotent. He was a corporate type, with a wife and kids who hated him, and he liked having this secret. You imagined that he felt almost as though a portion of his money, and therefore a portion of himself, had developed a life of its own, had sprung long, lovely legs and run out into the night. It must be nice for him to imagine what you were doing while he sat through long business meetings or as he suffered his family's stiff silence at the dinner table. You would call him every week to tell him about the parties you had been to, the people you had fucked, the food you had eaten, whether you felt tired or had stomach cramps or were planning to bleach your hair. You had come to enjoy these conversations. He was like a very low-maintenance friend, and you never felt that you had to be amusing with him; the exoticism of your age and situation imbued all the mundane details of your life with splendour.

What was strange, you felt, was that although he asked about your sex life, and occasionally wanted to know what you were wearing, you couldn't help noticing that your answers didn't excite him any more than when you talked him through the logistics of the week ahead. It was as if he asked these things in order to give himself an excuse that would mask the real, infinitely more complex erotic possibility you represented: that of living a different life, in a different body. Through you he could imagine what it might mean to move through the world as a focal point of desire, to have a life that unfolded in all directions at once, rather than one that had emptied away over the years until there was almost nothing left.

15

Inspired by your success, I set up a profile on the site you had used. There was a flurry of notifications almost immediately. Hello, sweetie, he messaged. You're a pretty baby. Where are you from? Send me a photo, sweetie. When I didn't reply for a few minutes, he followed up: Wanna facefuck?

It never did work out with my first suitor, but one of the next ones was promising. His name was Dave and in his profile he described himself as a light smoker, a social drinker, a married man and a millionaire. He also mentioned that he was a duke and that he was very handsome, but he hadn't uploaded any pictures so it was impossible to verify his claim. He sent me photos of handbags by Valentino: did I prefer the creamy pink in leather or the dark red in velvet? He called me princess, said what he wanted was to spoil me. Dave and I spoke a lot over the next week. He asked me strange questions. Was I an ugly child? Had I ever been to Berghain? How skinny were my thighs? Did I fantasise about women? His belief system, from what I could glean, was turbulent. He didn't like sluts, but he liked girls to be a little slutty. Bisexual women are the best women, he reckoned, but lesbians are ugly and evil. He liked feisty women, because it is a greater achievement to dominate them. He had many thoughts about women, but I began to doubt if he had ever really met one. He was fond of using the emoji of the smiley face with the tongue lolling out, but its meaning was unfixed. Sometimes it expressed innocent anticipation, such as when he was almost done with a day's work, and other times it dripped with sexual intent. For his faults, Dave showed some sensitivity when he talked about the comparative merits of different Valentino handbags (the chain, he felt, was more stylish than the strap, but he worried about my comfort). Still, the fact remained that I had been talking to him on and off for a week and none of these handbags had materialised.

16

When Dave and I parted ways, Fred was there to pick up the pieces. His profile read only: 'Middle-aged man seeks young girl'. I was charmed by his transparency. Seb1993 came sometime after Fred, though, truthfully, there may have been some overlap. Seb1993 did well to advertise his date of birth, his unique selling point. In pictures, he was remarkably attractive, even princely, though I wondered if my perspective had been warped by too many hours spent scrolling through innumerable toads. Seb1993 had a full head of dark, curly hair, a long, aristocratic nose with nostrils flared in slight disdain, sensuous lips and pale blue eyes. He called me cute, and baby. He sent me a video of him in his apartment in Barcelona, showing me the floral mosaic floors, the curved art-nouveau railings of the balcony outside his room and the sunny plaza underneath, with pigeons circling around the fountain. I should see it for myself sometime, he said casually. When I asked, he said he didn't use the site too much, that he preferred other dating apps, but that he occasionally tried it out because he was open to new experiences. Seb1993 seemed surprisingly normal, but it soon became apparent something was afoot. His register switched. Instead of cute and baby, he started to refer to me as good girl, which I felt did not bode well.

17

I was right. He was going to tie me down and tease me with his belt, he told me, unprompted. He would run the tip of his belt all over me and he would make me beg to be taken and I would do exactly what he told me to. I would do what he told me to until I cried, and if I didn't do exactly what he said, he would punish me hard, he would make me hurt. He wanted me to take a picture of myself wearing only underwear.

'You better look cute,' he threatened.

Apparently that day he was in a good mood, but he confessed, not to my great surprise, that he had a 'rough' side.

18

As the days went by, the men in the chats began to merge into one. I wondered if they were all different facets of the same demonic force, masquerading under different usernames. If all the threads did lead back to one solitary man in a dark room, I pictured him to be like Dennis Hopper playing Frank Booth in *Blue Velvet*, wheezing into a gas mask, torn between uncontrollable rage and crippling lust.

19

My financial situation was not helped by the fact that instead of finding a new job I had opted to spend my days talking to sordid strangers online.

20

It is people like you who give people like me a job, says the security guard philosophically in the small, brightly lit back room where I have been taken after he saw me on CCTV putting bottles of cider and white wine into my bag. Awkwardly, it was not just the bottles. I had also stolen, or attempted to steal: a platter of sushi, soy sauce, wasabi and ginger sachets, caramelised onion hummus, chicken strips, sliced gouda, three sesame bagels, blueberries, stuffed vine leaves, pastrami, black olives and a bar of almond chocolate; items which, as I take them out of my bag one by one and place them on the table under the security guard's unsmiling gaze, strike me as ridiculous, even offensive in their decadence. He fills out the familiar form and takes a mugshot of me, and once the administrative stuff is over he seems to soften towards me, and says, in a tone that is not unpaternal, 'I know how it is, everyone is poor', and gestures at the stack of identical forms that have built up on the table, twenty or thirty in a day. I wonder how many of them try wheedling, making excuses, telling tales of past woes, of hungry dependents, and how many take my approach: the barefaced lie. I have a receipt somewhere, I must have forgotten to print it, this is all a terrible misunderstanding. It doesn't work, but it is important to make some gesture towards your respective roles as squirming thief and stony security guard. To accept everything unprotestingly, to simply wait it out, would be quicker and more dignified, but it would reveal an unlikeable worldliness. It is better to be wide-eyed, slightly bewildered.

21

Had you found the only poor sucker on the vast internet who was willing to pour his money at the feet of a young woman in return for nothing?

22

Had you told me the whole truth, or had you, somewhere down the line, found yourself compromised, caught in a position where you felt indebted, or cornered into doing something you didn't want to do? Once you had become financially reliant on him, is it possible your sugar daddy had recovered from his supposed impotence? I know that when I probed, you seemed increasingly reluctant to talk about your arrangement, seeming bored by the whole subject. Had I accepted your unlikely story without scrutiny because I liked what it represented: sexiness tied up in toughness, arrogance, control?

23

The arguments in bars, drunk texts and late-night calls all blur together, but I remember the first breakup with perfect clarity because it was the only one that really mattered. After that, everything we did was just a footnote, a minor revision to a finished work. We were on a bench in St Stephen's Green in late October, leaves falling around us. You rolled compact cigarettes, which you smoked quickly, avoiding my eyes, flicking the ash to the ground with sharp taps. I had prepared a careful trap, but you sidestepped it and I fell in instead.

'Maybe this isn't worth the hassle,' I threatened.

To my surprise, you only shrugged and said 'Maybe', and that was the end.

24

I remembered Jean Rhys's conviction that a new room is a new life, but I had forgotten her conclusion. 'Never tell the truth about this business of rooms, because it would bust the roof off everything and undermine the whole social system. All rooms are the same. All rooms have four walls, a door, a window or two, a bed, a chair . . . Why should I worry about changing my room?' There is a serenity that can be reached by admitting defeat.

Caterpillar

CLARE FISHER

You would like to tell a story about your body and how it is not real. You would like to tell a story that feels real in the way your body would feel real were your body a real body. The problem is, you don't know how to tell stories that feel real in the way bodies feel real because all your body feels is other peoples' bodies and the stories that they tell about them. The problem is, you mistake such stories for your own. The problem is, you shove such mistakes between the exam certificates in the bottom drawer of the filing cabinet in the back room of the house in which you grew not-up. The problem is, you grew not-up. The problem is, these problems don't make the sorts of problems that make a story, and even if they, by some magic, did, you couldn't make them into some other, more real body, because bodies aren't made out of stories, they are made out of things like fat like white blood cells like snot like bones like eyelashes like elbow wrinkles like blood that looks like snot but black. The problem is, these things are tangled with un-things like verbs like feelings like verbs which do things with feelings like make your cheeks sting whenever you remember that your memory of being a boy is not a memory in the way that your friends voting you the ugliest girl is. The problem is, if this problem is neither a body nor a story, then what kind of problem are you? All you can say for sure is that the filing cabinet was red like a tomato that refuses to ripen.

You would like to tell a story about your body, and how it is not real because it is your cousin Ben's body. Specifically, it is your cousin Ben's body as he practices karate, swiping at the air between his body and the body of your mum and his mum, who are sisters, which means they both came out of their mum's body, which is weird, when you think about it, which you mostly don't, just like you mostly don't think about pooing, and how everyone does it, even famous people, like Julie Andrews, who plays Maria in *The Sound of Music*, which you watch every night before bed.

But it's not the story of how you need the story that is Julie Andrews rescuing seven rich orphans from loneliness and motherlessness and even the Nazis that you wanted to tell; it's the story of your cousin and how his karate suit is so white it scorches the back of your eyeball. You see it when you go to sleep in your aunt's squeaky spare bed. You see it when you wake up to the sound of your mums' voices crashing into each other. You see it when your mum bundles you, still pyjamaed, into a taxi. You see it in the open-mouthed silence that is your mum's response to the question of when you will next visit.

Your own pyjamas are blue and red and yellow with tiny black tractors all over them, but if you turn them inside out they are almost white, and when you leap around your mum's house it feels almost as big as your aunt's house, and your arms almost as long as Ben's.

So eccentric, your mum says, when she understands that the inside-out pyjamas have become another of your habits.

You do not tell her why you wear them inside out. You do not tell any one. The not-telling makes the feeling that turning your pyjamas inside out will make the feeling that your body is Ben's body more real. The not-telling is a spell. Ta-da.

You would like to tell a story about your body and how it is not real because it is your dad's body, because why else would you feel so empty when he goes to work? You carry your Donald Duck lunchbox the way he carries his briefcase. You draw pictures of the stories he tells you about when he was a boy. The stories are mostly happy stories; the pictures contain things like kites and rope swings and houses and climbing frames and bicycles, as well as boys. When the stories are finished, you fold and staple the paper so that it looks like a book. You feel the opposite of empty, which may or may not be what other people mean when they say 'happy'. You feel the way the boy must've felt in those stories. It is almost as if, in drawing him, you have become him.

You would like to tell a story about your body and how it is not a body but a filing cabinet which, unlike the filing cabinet in the front room of the house in which you grew not-up, unlike any of the grey filing cabinets you've seen at school, unlike any of the filing cabinets existing in the world, is not real. You know it is not real because it can do things that neither bodies nor filing cabinets are supposed to do, such as store your mum's feelings.

Your mum's feelings are more real than anybody else's feelings; they are fleshy like the hunks of meat the two of you don't eat at Liz and Rob's barbecue. You eat a bun stuffed with cheese and salad and crisps. The cheese does not look or taste real. You are on the verge of working out what it does taste like when your mum's shrieks flood your ears, your mouth, your nostrils. She is waving her hands and shouting at Rob. She does not like Rob. You know this because she tells you everything she thinks, and a lot of what she thinks is about men, and how Bad they are – almost as Bad as sugar and meat.

There is a plastic taste in your mouth: it's hot and tight in there, and whether it's the cheese or the guilt, you do not know; the only knowable thing right now is that you've failed.

You did not lock your drawers and now your mum's feelings are everywhere

everyone

is quiet

even Rob   is quiet

they are looking   at her mouth

how it opens and shuts and opens and shuts and

the sound   spills out   and out and   out

they look confused and sad and scared, very scared.

But you're not scared, you can't be. You know she is only doing what she is doing because of what she says happened to her when she was a child and what her sisters say did not; you know that the difference between these two words, 'do' and 'not' is the reason you will never visit your aunt's house, never see your cousin Ben in his karate uniform ever again. What you don't know is how her sisters can be sure of what did or didn't happen to her when they have not been in her body, not once. You have, though. You lived there for a whole nine months. Now, watching Ben and Liz and Carry and Rachel and Fred and all the other people holding their paper plates of black-red meat and creamy white potato salad and mustard dots and sausages that look like sun-burnt fingers, looking at your mum as if she is the Bad – you're sure. It happened. The thing her sisters said never happened. The Bad. It's real. It's in you. It is you. You wish it wasn't, but it is. You wish you could scream too.

'I think you should leave,' Liz says.

'Right,' says your mum. 'Right, so I'm the bad person now, am I? I am always the bad person. Fuck you.' She is crying and making strange hiccupping sounds. Her face looks like someone else's face. This thing that traps the two of you – blows hole after hole in any sort of us you try to make with other people – isn't her. It's a monster. A ghost. And you, you should be better at keeping it in the filing cabinet. You should possibly get a lock for the filing cabinet or push the filing cabinet into a high-security bank vault. Yes. Yes, you need to be better at being what you are, that's what.

'I'm sorry. God, I'm sorry.'

By the time you get home, her face looks like her face again. Your dad is in the back room – the room where the filing cabinet is not – watching telly with his T-shirt rolled up over his round hairy belly.

'That was quick,' he says.

You say nothing. Your mum says nothing. But even though his body is mostly in a place where yours and hers are not, he hears it.

'Oh,' he said. 'Blow your top, did you?' Wrong question. Wrong question.

'I did *not*,' she says, '*blow my top*.'

And then that's it. They're fighting again. And so you run upstairs, away from their feelings, away from their voices, into your bedroom. You shut your bedroom door and turn on your current favourite story tape: *The Secret Garden*. It is about a girl called Mary Lennox. She is an orphan. It is sad, very sad, to be an orphan, and it's not that you want your parents to die, but sometimes, sometimes, especially in their never-ending fights, you wish they would. Mary could say, 'My parents are dead', and then she could act all moody and rude, and people would think, *She is moody and rude*, but they wouldn't mind too much because you're allowed to be moody and rude when your parents are dead. If you said, 'My parents are alive but they are not very good at staying in their bodies, they aren't really adults, and I have to work hard to stop their feelings making a hole in time and space and people and everything all of the time', people would laugh and say: 'My, what an overactive imagination you have.'

You would like to tell a story about your body and how it is not

You would like to tell a story about your body and how it is not real because it is your best friend Freya's body. You know, of course, that this is impossible, but if Jesus, whom you must learn about at school, can be both alive and dead, and if your mum can believe one story about what her dad did to her when she was smaller than you while her sisters believe a completely different story, and if you have to squeeze your body into the gap between the two stories when you go to visit your aunt, on the train, alone, you don't see why you shouldn't have a little impossibility of your own.

Freya doesn't know about these stories, nor do any of the other kids at school; sometimes you think this is why you are the only one who prefers division and subtraction to the games and dressing-up corner. But the more likely explanation is that you are a grown-up trapped in a child's body. Yes, this is why you feel more like the cardboard your mum is forever trying to squash into the recycling bin than like the blond-haired girls in books. Which is why you want to grow big and tall and fast. You want to grow until your mum's story feels as unreal as the body that is not quite your body does now.

Until then, however, you must make your body look more like Freya's body by wearing the same yellow dress to the Easter fair. Freya doesn't know this, of course; she thinks you are wearing yellow so that you can run around, pretending to be baby chicks. So, when you see her by the raffle table in black leggings and a pink jumper you feel worse than when that boy kicked you in the fanny. Your chest gets loud and sticky. You walk towards her. You walk towards her knowing that she is not you, that you are never going to be any one but you, and you can't bear it, you cannot bear it, and whether it is this feeling that makes you spill Freya's hot chocolate all over her mum's pale pink skirt, you do not know.

'It was an accident,' you say, over and over, to your mum, as she shouts at you on the way home. Your mum doesn't know what is happening in your not-real body, but she knows these words aren't true.

'Enough!' she says.

When you lay down on the pavement because you couldn't get your haircut in the barber, it was terrible, but you were two, and two-year-olds are meant to be terrible. She has told you this story many times; how, when she pushed the buggy past the barber's, you threw your arms into the air and yelled, 'Mine!' You wouldn't stop, so she went in and asked if they'd cut your hair.

'No,' said the barber, 'but you can get her hair cut in the women's hairdresser's next door.'

But you did not want your hair cut in the women's hairdresser's next door. You did not want it so badly that you laid down on the pavement and screamed and kicked. You were smaller than you are now, but too big for your mum to lift you and the shopping and the buggy up by herself. People did not help, and then an old drunk held the buggy so that she could bundle you into a taxi. By the time it dropped you off at home, you were smiling and laughing – almost as if you had nothing to do with what had just happened.

Your mum often tells this story to other adults. She tells them so that they'll laugh, which they do, especially if you're wearing a frilly dress, which you often are. You laugh, too; you want them to think that you've grown out of wanting to be in other people's bodies. You haven't, though. You just do it more quietly than before, and only with girls.

When you get back to your house, your mum does not unlock the door. She stands on the front step and grips your shoulders. 'So, what do you think? Are you ready to act like a proper seven-year-old? No more tantrums?'

The wind blows your skirt against your fanny, which starts to itch, and you want to scratch it but you can't. You have to act as if you don't even have one, which is how all adults must act, especially women – you often see men walk down the street with their hands down their pants but no one tells them off – and so you just hop from one foot to the other.

'Yes.'

You're not ready, not at all, but you are clever. You are clever because you need to solve the problem of your not-body the way other people need food, and if the answers you've found so far have turned out to be wrong, it doesn't matter; you will find more. Besides, you want to go inside and take off your stupid dress.

You would like to tell a story about your body and how it is not real because it is not a human body but the body of a caterpillar – specifically, the one in the picture book *The Very Hungry Caterpillar* by Eric Carle.

The very hungry caterpillar eats one apple on Monday, two pears on Tuesday, three plums on Wednesday, four strawberries on Thursday and five oranges on Friday. Each day, he is bigger and hungrier than the day before. On Saturday he eats chocolate cake, an ice-cream cone, a pickle, a slice of Swiss cheese, a slice of salami, a lollipop, a cherry pie, a sausage, a cupcake and a watermelon. On Sunday he eats one green leaf; at last, he is full. He builds himself a little brown house, where he sleeps. He wakes up a beautiful butterfly. Ta-da!

The difference between you and the book caterpillar is that you will never get to Sunday: you will never wake up a beautiful butterfly. At eleven, you know this the same way you know the word 'girl' is the most nonsense of all the words; you like to mutter it until it resembles the scraps of tissues that fall out of your school bag.

For the first ten years of your life, you ate the way the caterpillar ate on the weekdays. You ate this way because sweets were Bad and your mum was Good for giving you wholemeal sandwiches and Salt 'n' Shake crisps without the salt, and rice cakes and sugarless carrot cake, instead. You liked these things; you really did. But now you want to eat chocolate cake and ice cream and lollipops and ice cream and ice cream more ice cream more. Time is now divided into the time you are eating sweet things and the time you are not.

You're never full, not even when your stomach physically hurts: no way would you could you do with just one leaf.

You think about this while you are reading *The Very Hungry Caterpillar* to the toddlers next door. When you are done, their mum offers you a chocolate eclair. You eat it so quickly you don't taste it. As you are about to finish a second, she says: 'Oh, enjoy those hollow legs, you won't have them forever.'

Your own mum said something similar when you bought that mini skirt last week; she is always reminding you that you will soon 'fill out'. She's wrong, though. They all are. Because in your body, it will be Saturday forever.

You would like to tell a story about your body and how it feels the most real in the future – specifically the one in which you have boobs and your period. You know all about periods from your mum and from books and from Lia, a girl in your class who curls up on the changing-room benches and clutches her stomach and refuses to do PE. Some days you feel a wetness down there and you think: *This is it, at last, the beginning of my real life.* But it is only that white stuff that is slushing out of you pretty much all the time, and you try not to think about it, you do, but it's hard. The older you get the more things there are to not-think about.

You would like to tell a story about your body and how – but no, there is no past, no future, no time in which it feels real, but especially not in the 'now' in which your period starts.

Your period starts without your permission.

Your period starts, even though you have barely, as your mum threatened, 'filled out', and your boobs are not boobs are just glorified nipples.

Your period starts as a brown stain, then continues as a thick red-black-purple gush that is nothing like any of the stories anyone has told you about periods.

Your period soaks through a supersized pad within the hour. You ask to go to the toilet in Chemistry, but the teacher, Mr Croon, who thinks he is cool because his ties are adorned with grinning Bart Simpsons, says no. You change it between lessons, but then you're late for Geography, and Miss Braithwaite tells you off.

'I expected better from you,' she says, and you are sure that she and everyone can smell it hear it feel it trickling out of this thing that cannot be you. You look at the boys, who are looking at the dicks they can't stop Tipp-Ex-ing on each other's pencil cases, and you want to smash them.

Your mum is kind. She buys you a 500ml tub of Häagen-Dazs Belgian chocolate ice cream and lets you take the next day off school. While she is at work you lie around in your pyjamas, waiting for this body to turn into some other body, the body you were meant to have – that's really real. But it keeps glooping out and out and out and out and out and out and you hate it you hate it how will you live your life like this

how?

To escape this question you finally start the essay you've spent two weeks putting off. It's about that Robert Browning poem, 'Porphyria's Lover', in which the male narrator murders his girlfriend by strangling her with her own hair. You don't want to write, you don't want to read, but you do, and nothing happens, and nothing happens, and nothing happens – and then it is as if you are peeping into the whatever that is behind the poem. Magic. Ta-da.

'How are you doing?'

It isn't until your mum gets home that you realise that you've gone at least three hours without thinking about blood or ice cream or the lunch that was impossible to eat, over there, in the place behind the words; it's dark outside, and your skull feels wobbly on your neck.

'Better,' you say. 'Much better.'

She asks if you fancy takeaway pizza, and you say, 'Yes.' You shove it into your mouth three slices at a time as if you have just finished a long hike, which you have, sort of.

You would like to—

Yes. You would, actually.

You would like to tell a story about your body and how it is not real, and how the only thing that makes the feeling that it is not real feel bad in a way that feels good is eating less than it needs.

At fifteen, you go from eating like the very hungry caterpillar on Saturday to the weekday caterpillar; you eat leaves and berries and tomatoes and more leaves. At first, it's hard. You alternate between periods of leaf-eating and periods of ice cream pizza Mini Rolls hummus Kettle chips ice cream everything everything everything forever. But you can do hard things. You can become a filing cabinet for other people's feelings; you can get up extra early every morning to practice Maths GCSE. You can, even though you are not a Maths person, get a A*.

You can make yourself into any sort of person.

You can! And you do.

And by the end of the summer holidays it's easy. You don't even want to eat Mini Rolls and bagels and pizzas and cakes and crisps at sleepovers. When your friends ask are you really not hungry, you can honestly shake your head no. Because your hunger is dead. You killed it. You killed it, and in its space is something like the feeling you used to get when you used to get stoned with the friends who aren't really your friends any more. It makes you feel floaty and fizzy, as if your body is real but that's OK, because it's not a body, it's a gummy cola bottle, and someone is slowly chewing it down. It's your secret. Magic. Ta-da.

You would like to tell a story about your body, and how it is not real because it is your boyfriend's body, which is smaller and thinner and tauter than yours. Despite this, it sweats less and has a lot less hair. You know that your body cannot really be your boyfriend's body because he is a boy and you are a girl; because his parents were born in Vietnam and yours in the UK; because he is him and you are you; because the only body you are ever going to live in is the one you are already not-living in and why is this so much harder to grasp than Maths A-Level? You don't know.

Strangers often shout in the street: 'Hey! You're taller than him!'

He hates it, you half-hate it half-like it; what you hate is the idea that men have to be taller than women; what you like is the idea, crouching in the underbelly of the first, that because you are taller than him you are more of a man than him. Not that you want to be a man; you actually feel quite sorry for them. Sure, they get to do what they want and no one tells them off for it, but there are things they can't know, even the clever ones – especially the clever ones. It's more that when your boyfriend looks at the parts of you that make you look like a girl, you feel like a mistake.

You would like to tell a story about your body and how it is not real because

~~because~~

~~because~~

~~be~~

TechNoWhere

LIAM CAGNEY

1

Techno is the art of nowhere.

Techno is a musical art for those who feel like they're nowhere all the time: when they're on the top deck of a bus, or shopping in the overlit aisles of a supermarket, or laying their head down on the pillow and staring up at the ceiling:

nowhere at all these times, yet somehow inexplicably *there* all the same.

Techno affirms the reality of this nowhere.

Within the club's darkness – through immersion in flickering lights and out-there sounds and rhythms like insect heartbeats – techno envelops you in silence. Then, techno whispers that, yes, what you feel despite it all *is* real, that history is madness and selfhood a fantasy.

Nowhere and nothing become synonymous. Neither term is negative: on the contrary, nothing and nowhere are joyous affirmation, what remains when everything is wiped away, beyond all personhood and place.

The techno club at its best stages the nothing and the nowhere. The dancefloor darkness is an inscrutable zone, a liberating non-place, a space that's neither inside nor outside.

It's no coincidence techno clubs are found in no-man's lands. Industrial units and basements are history's border. They are where the new first appears – ominous, glamorous – a place for the alien, the other.

Techno always comes from aliens.

From Detroit to Dusseldorf, Tokyo to Sheffield, techno was born of marginal types:

born of the community of those who don't fit in;

born of the community of those without a community;

born of freaks;

born of loners;

born of those, like you, in thrall to the nothing.

2

These were my thoughts that muggy summer morning at the Berlin techno club Berghain – thoughts raging like a hillside of foxglove and ferns in a hurricane – as my body sat cowering in a dank toilet cubicle, taking refuge from the abject madness into which my morning had devolved – trying in vain, as so often, to think myself out of trouble.

I had come to Berghain that morning excitedly but without expectations, accompanied, improbably, by the tall, polo-clad Jürgen, a Dutch neolib economist I barely knew. Jürgen had spent the preceding Saturday night, as we toured Kreuzberg's dive bars, praising the free market and iPhones and dating apps. He was full of himself. I was hanging out with my friend David, a bohemian economist of whom Jürgen was an old acquaintance, and being your classic boojie desperate to get past Berghain's famously stringent bouncers Jürgen pricked up his ears when I mentioned that I had two Berghain guestlist spots for that night. And when David, my expected plus one, fell ill and went home, our unwelcome club date was sealed.

To make things more complicated, it wasn't actually me who was on the guestlist: it was my Scottish football-hooligan friend

John (he was dating Berghain's accountant). But since I knew John wasn't going, I had prudently decided to assume John's identity at the door.

All of which should have been fine. Except that, at 5 a.m., under a radiant firmament of summer blue, as Jürgen, in his Louis Vuitton jacket and preppy chinos, and I, in my unkempt T-shirt, stood on the gravel before Berghain's hulking mountain, eyed by the moustachioed muscular bouncer with his clipboard, my vision began to shimmer. The mushrooms I had been idly microdosing earlier that night had gone rogue: they had gone *macro*. A lysergic tint washed over me; my tongue thickened; and I fumbled. When asked my name, I mistakenly blurted not the guestlist name but my own name.

I'd been mooching around Berlin a month or so by this point, a recent musicology graduate – an overqualified dropout. I was well enough acquainted with Berghain not to have bothered going there for years. I'd first been as a student in 2006, and in 2010 had first kissed an eyelinered blond woman there, Emma, who for a few years after became my life partner in crime. I already knew the gothic concrete, the brute gay energy firing the ex-thermal energy plant's industrial corridors and stairwells, already knew the excess, the genderfuck, the drug lunacy, the endless opening hours. For years Berghain had held little interest – I assumed that clubbing had been a fixture of my early twenties, whereas now, a hard-won PhD under my belt, I'd moved on to more respectable things. I was paid to review operas and write classical music programme notes.

But my clubbing past up till then had been merely a prologue.

Jürgen sighed dramatically. 'That was worse than the border crossing into Israel,' he muttered as we passed the security check and paid the cashier. After the bouncer had asked me my name and I replied 'Liam – I mean John!', and following a stern stare and Jürgen shifting his feet, and an excruciating moment of deliberation, we were waved in, skipping with relief past a queue of black-clad hopefuls that stretched off for miles.

A Bavarian musicologist friend, Karin, had given me the shrooms as part payment for a copyediting job I'd done (yes, how very Berlin), suggesting that gentle microdosing might help my depression and dissociation. The shrooms were an ungodly synthetic crossbreed of Mexican psilocybin and some unnamed species, and, as I discovered, this singular hybrid granted you all the awesomely intense visuals with none of the comforting giggles.

By the time Jürgen and I left our things at Berghain's coat check and, passing a statue colossus, began ascending the vast iron staircase up to the club proper on the first floor – from which darkness the brutal pounding techno kindled our excitement – it had become abundantly clear that, through my drunken hands, I had fucked up the whole microdosing thing: I had tasted and tested too much. My dread rose with each wobbly step up that stairwell. I gazed in dilated-eye wonder at the pillars of purple light shooting off and felt shock at the sound system's oceanic roar, knowing full well I was hurtling headlong into a full-on psychedelic trip, in the most trip-uncongenial of settings.

We quickly decamped to the mellower upstairs Panorama Bar. But the red halogen strip lights ululated; the music's jazzy piano morphed into android laughter; my left hand's fingers stretched away like fleshy measuring tapes; not to mention the overwhelming purpleness of the gender-fluid Prince lookalike before the DJ box, or the deafening cigarette smoke swirling round the two bald red-kimono lesbians dancing together in silky synch, and my heart pounded, and it was all too much. Berghain meant sensory overload – reality turned up to eleven.

I began panicking. I desperately needed some respite, desperately needed silence, desperately needed grounding contact with comforting normality. But when I turned to tell Jürgen, he was gone: now that we were inside, this smarmy neolib had ditched me. I was alone with my terror.

That's how I ended up cowering in a metallic toilet cubicle. There was nowhere else in Berghain where you could get a break from the sensory onslaught. I was trapped in a madness machine with my mind amplifying everything a hundredfold.

3

My encounters with techno up till this point had been few and casual. In the 1990s, in our rural Donegal bedroom, our nearest neighbour a kilometre away, my beanie-hatted older brother Éamonn had exposed me to rave and ambient music. As an adult I'd drifted into playing in noise bands and eventually did a PhD on post-war French electroacoustic music. In my spare time during my London grad student years, as my longterm relationship with Emma disintegrated, I often whiled away time dreaming on the sounds of Drexciya or Plastikman or Underground Resistance.

I knew about techno's history. I knew that when club techno arose in 1980s Detroit – America's first deindustrialised city – Black producers were reimagining their urban environment as a site of futurist fantasies. Cybotron's dystopian 1984 track 'Techno City', one of the first to foreground that term, was inspired by Fritz Lang's *Metropolis* and the Tokyo of Yellow Magic Orchestra's earlier track 'Technopolis'. 'I extrapolated the necessity of interfacing the spirituality of human beings into the cybernetic matrix,' said Cybotron's Rik Davis, 'between the brain, the soul and the mechanisms of cyberspace.' As well as the music, techno meant a whole conceptual vision – a post-human vision not unlike that of Donna Haraway's contemporary *Cyborg Manifesto*. 'The cyborg would not recognise the Garden of Eden,' Haraway wrote in a feminist context. 'It is not made of mud and cannot dream of returning to dust.'

Jeff Mills, who pretty much invented modern club techno, similarly spoke of shedding his human form through music. 'I'm becoming the third person,' he told *The Wire*, comparing his productions to robot probes of alien territories. Along with Mike Banks, Mills was co-founder of the Detroit techno collective Underground Resistance (UR). UR sought to harness techno's power of anonymity to de-programme people from the 'dominant mindbeam': the false reality by which, through mass media, we're conditioned to accept an untrue sense of who we are. 'Everything you see may not be real,' UR sang on their 1998 album *Interstellar Fugitives*: 'It might be a mirage.'

4

In my tripping state I leaned my elbows on the bar's glass counter; the contact made liquid ripples. Around me the walls were charnel-house black. The sensory barrage remained relentless and overwhelming. I hoped a shot of Jäger would take the edge off the psychedelics.

Berghain's gay clones and butch queens seemed like emissaries from the future. Beside me was a characteristically bizarre trio. One of them was a haggard white SO36 punk with a red mohawk; dressed in red tartan, he swayed woozily on his Doc Martens. The second, steadying him, was a topless Black woman; I admired her spangly gold hoop earrings, though her snakelike green hair extensions gave her the aspect of a gorgon. The third was a toking East Asian-looking man with a bare chest, baggy white cargo pants and a ludicrous Dali moustache.

Did I look that weird, too? Or, on the contrary, did I look *sufficiently* weird?

It was as if, in this club, pushed to the limit – humans at the limit of being human, music at the limit of being music – everything was finally revealed as it truly was; like I was being granted a vision of life in its monstrous nudity. That was what this club was, I thought, as a sweet smell filled my nose, a vast black box, where—

'Toke?' the East Asian man asked kindly: he was brandishing his magic wand to me with Salvador Dali realness.

I shook my head. 'I don't take drugs, thanks.'

Under the glass counter, what had at first glance appeared to be a row of glowing rotisserie chickens on closer inspection proved to be a debauched amber sculpture: running the length of the seedy bar, it showed a series of recumbent bald male clones, naked, making love. The dancefloor was full of those hyper-masculine types – brawny, poppers-sniffing and near molten.

Berghain, with its fathomless corridors and experiential intensity, was like an immersive artwork. Berghain's founders, Michael Teufele and Norbert Thormann, had reportedly said something to that effect to the DJ and writer Daniel Wang back in 2004, the first time they showed off their new club to friends. The owners 'stated that they wanted to create a club as a work of art', Wang said, as I'd read before online.

I connected this to what the 1920s Russian Formalists had written about art. The artwork exists to explode our world's narcotic everyday fug, said the Russian formalist Viktor Shklovsky. It does this through the act of defamiliarization:

> Art exists that one may recover the sensation of life; it exists to make one feel things, to make the stone stony. The purpose of art is to impart the sensation of things as they are perceived and not as they are known. The technique of art is to make objects 'unfamiliar' . . .

In our everyday life, the engine of normality is habit. You learn to put on one shoe and then another; you learn to take the train to work, to have the same conversations as others at the water cooler, to go on the same holidays as everyone else, to buy the same vacuous consumer goods. 'Habitualisation', wrote Shklovsky, 'devours work, clothes, furniture, one's wife, and the fear of war.'

Berghain served up life defamiliarised, life rendered in its true strangeness. Perhaps this techno club, this colossal black box, signalled a new form of art, with nameless electronic sounds at its core.

5

Back on the dancefloor my state of panic peaked. Far away through the nighttime forest of bodies, I knew the DJ currently playing was called Function, techno royalty. Yet he appeared to me in the DJ box like an imperious stag with yellow fur and luminous green antlers.

The techno he played was way too big, the lights way too streaming, my fingers way too long. All of it was beyond me. It was a profoundly disturbing yet elating experience that, in the end, I only got through when I realised that, rather than try to escape it, I had to embrace it. I internally repeated to myself Nietzsche's stoic mantra *amor fati*: love of one's fate. Love all of this. Submit to this experience unreservedly and in every fibre.

Do with me what you will.

With this, the peaking state magically evened out. I merged with my dancefloor surroundings; I found composure, relief – even joy. Delirious but lucid, I was swept along in the hypnotic techno to which the thousandfold revellers around me, naked or in fetish gear, were oscillating their tattooed limbs.

I was finally at ease enough to listen to the music properly. Function's bare pounding kick drum pulse sounded steady and alone, drawing in your ear to its periodicity. Gradually over this, an explosive, harmonically rich bass note was resounding, once every two bars. The huge bass note's resonant decay flowed slowly out, expansive and tidal, to submerge this hall, fusing your body to the expanse of teeming nothingness.

As in much modernist music, everything recognisably musical was stripped away: no melody, no harmony, no verse or chorus, no formal structure, nothing that could contain or pin down the electricity of the sound itself, which poured all over us like a roaring river of intoxicating wine. The music's goal, achieved through extreme repetition, seemed to be to strip away everything historically determined – in other words, sullied by having been assigned an identity – and to let sound resound in its true voracious anonymity, its core nothingness, unconstrained by musical forms.

After a while, I leaned back against the latticework barrier spanning the back of Berghain's dancefloor. Behind me was a fall of twenty metres, down to the concrete ground level and the Dionysian threshold guardian statue. I arched my head up.

Red laser lights were making slow sweeps as on a painted canvas, flickering and configuring into polygons. Then at once the laser lights turned blue. And the room, too, full of dry ice, turned blue. And staring at the boundless static blue, I had the sense of my individuality evaporating. And I was united with the blue and with the droning bass, pouring out of myself through my eyes, pouring out of myself through my ears, pouring out of myself through myself, becoming the faint scintillations, becoming the space between things, becoming the brilliant nothing.

It was annihilation, if you like – merging with the nothing, here in this staged nowhere. But it wasn't pessimistic: I united with the too-small, the granular, the particles and energy fields subsisting through all tangible things but which are always usually erased. Things belong to the human scale; on the micro scale, the nothing proliferates freely in endless iterative series, undulating in every direction, with neither centre nor subject – yet no less real for all that. It felt like the experience I had at Tate Modern before a Rothko canvas when, having stared at it for half an hour, I abruptly found myself *become* the canvas; since for your vision and your audition, there is no absolute frame of reference, no changeless object, only eternally ongoing becoming and voidedness. It briefly shows you that a universe subsists outside your body with which, through the artwork, moving beyond the tyranny of personhood, you can be united.

All of which is very high flown indeed. And all of which disappeared, like a dream upon waking, the moment I shakily stepped back outside that grand Soviet building.

There I stood, dazed in the squint-eyed afternoon light. I shuffled past the hundreds of bodies queuing outside the club (so many, so many). I unlocked from the wire fence the rickety bike Jürgen had gifted me in exchange for the guestlist. I briefly thought of Jürgen, who before leaving I had spotted near the toilets but decided to ignore, sat as he was with protruding jaw between two men whom he was telling about his experience of love on a recent corporate Ayahuasca trip.

Then, I cycled all the way back to my home in a Weißensee squat, out on the city's northern edge. The tree-fringed streets and redbrick buildings rose to meet me, glowing as if they were in on the whole thing.

6

Few things are more tedious than a drug memoir – someone droning on about how wasted he got in Berlin. For this brand of storytelling, I love the catty phrase with which Carl Solomon, dedicatee of Allen Ginsberg's poem 'Howl', dismissed Ginsberg's Beat epic: 'crypto-bohemian boasting á la Rimbaud'.

I open with a tripping anecdote not to boast or vice signal. The drugs were only a catalyst for taking off my blinkers and seeing a wide vista of life I'd ignored. That summer weekend, techno entered my life more or less unannounced, a Doppelgänger that from then on began following me around and mimicking my movements. Eventually I took notice and wisely resolved to follow it. Because maybe *it* was the original and I was the copy.

7

It was a time in my life when I was looking for something. I had arrived in Berlin that July for a long summer break. Ireland had exhausted me and I'd exhausted Ireland. I was disillusioned, depressed and lost. I had no stable job and few remaining prospects. I was no longer young, my academic career had been stillborn, and I ended up in Berlin simply because I'd lived there a few years earlier and knew the lay of the land.

I rented a room in a remarkably bizarre place even by Berlin standards – a huge former Stasi base called the ECC. Looming up high from grey industrial storage yards, the ECC had a House of Usher vibe, an uncanny artefact of a dead past. Inside, it comprised hundreds of rooms, most of them empty, linked by echoing stairwells and fathomless corridors. It housed artists and students, anarchists and Syrian refugees, assorted lost souls and me. One day in the basement, one of my fellow tenants, a ponytailed Spanish guitarist, found filing cabinets full of old Stasi files on DDR citizens. Something like that happened every day.

My studio you might call ruin chic: a threadbare carpet, no curtains, exposed piping, sparse furniture. A decades-lingering smell of industrial cleaning products filled my nose each morning, and at night I lay awake staring at the piping, wondering what I was doing there. I listened to Natalie Dessay singing Mozart arias to buoy myself. Bursts of laughter resounded down the corridor of traumatised Syrian men playing videogames. I felt disoriented. How had I come to be nowhere?

When I invited my punk friend Barry out there for dinner one evening, he casually remarked that the building had 'a stench of death' about it. Barry wasn't wrong. In a storage space beside my room lay the unclaimed possessions of a young woman who had died at the ECC, whose body supposedly hadn't been discovered for weeks. Among her leftover possessions were disturbed pen drawings, a Sinead O'Connor biography, and a black-and-white photo of her smiling with a boyfriend. In an empty studio one evening a few of us gave her a makeshift posthumous art exhibition.

David, my economist friend, also lived at the ECC. And it was David who urged me to take another look at Berghain. He insisted the club owners wanted someone like me to write about clubbing – to take it seriously. I brooded on this. 'The thing about Berghain,' he said, 'is that it's all about the music – it's not the hedonism but the music that comes first'.

8

If techno was the art of nowhere, as I'd been inspired to think – a musical art for those who feel like they're nowhere all of the time – how could such an art have any form at all? Wouldn't the art of nowhere be destined to be inchoate and formless?

Jeff Mills's DJ sets, through their frenetic mixing and relentless intensity, generate a sort of organised delirium. On his classic mix album *Live at the Liquid Room*, recorded in 1995 at a dingy Tokyo club, Mills weaves a continuous texture through micro-modifications to perceptual units, layering successive vinyl records and loops within each record. (Mills mixes mostly his own productions on *Live at the Liquid Room*'s first segment.) Accelerated over a steady beat, recognisable sound elements are transmitted so as to become an unfamiliar delirious stream.

As in the contemporaneous films of Martin Arnold such as *Pièce Touchée*, where fierce repetition of micro-second segments subverts the dreary dominion of domesticated time, Mills's deranged repetitions open a different sense of time. Mills sounds gritty, and occasionally it reminds me of looking at a person in a photograph and seeing not only the face but the cracks and flaws, part of the image's vitality. In Mills's music, it's the perceptual unit that's being composed, corroded and radiant. Mills's febrile sound is built on scrambled everyday elements, witnessed from some nowhere which his music accesses.

Drexciya's techno, by contrast, was more introverted. Each record by James Stinson and Gerald Donald in their Drexciya guise – or by their many alter egos (Der Zyklus, Abstract Thought, Japanese Telecom . . .) – is like a musical signal sent from an imaginary universe. Where Mills's DJing is expansive and quickening, Drexciya's music, particularly their late-period music, is contemplative. Albums like *The Opening of the Cerebral Gate* and *Grava IV* at base explored the fundamental disjunction of subjectivity, between outer identity (the everyday world) and inner universe (the anonymous, the nowhere).

In his final interview before his young death, James Stinson, who invented the Drexciya concept, described their music as 'an infinite journey to inner space within'. The music's aim was 'to find the beauty that's inside and bring it out.' Drexciya's narrative concept on *Grava IV*, of a return by Afro-diasporic mutants to their true home not on the earth but in the stars, resonated with earlier music of the Black Atlantic, such as Bob Marley and the Wailers' *Exodus*. But it also had wider application, a dualism whose tension is felt by the marginalized of all types. On this earth, you are always at once both here and nowhere.

9

I had gone through life feeling like someone pretending to be a person. Where some faked their own death, I faked my own life. Adulthood had presented a catalogue of my shortcomings: not academic enough to be academic, not Irish enough to be Irish, not straight enough to be straight, not queer enough to be queer, not working class enough to be working class, not middle class enough to be middle class. I realised that that was part of what a techno club touched on. This darkness, this sensory deprivation, this cut with the everyday world: they allowed you to meditate on your non-self – that is, on your true being.

When I returned to Berghain in the weeks and months and years afterwards, I did so *to get a dose of reality*. The everyday world is strange already; being a person with a name is alienating already. Berghain's club environment exaggerates that strangeness to the furthest degree, such that the everyday starts to stretch and tear apart and show what's underneath: to let you feel at one with the strangeness, at home in the nowhere.

Trespasses at Park House

YARA RODRIGUES FOWLER

‘Trespass’:

entry onto private property without the permission of its owner

or

a moral sin committed against a person.

■

Some questions I have:

Who owns the land? And

Who is beating their wives?

‘HALL OF FAME? Tragic tale of abandoned mansion left to rot – can you guess the VERY famous figure who called it home?’
The Sun, 31 August 2022

There was once a family of landowners.

The monarch of their country made them into aristocrats.

■

There was once another family of landowners.

They lent money to the rulers of their country and helped them fight wars in other countries.

In exchange, the monarch of their country made them into aristocrats.

■

According to the laws of that country, the first-born son of a family should inherit the land and other wealth of that family.

The purpose of these laws was to prevent the land and other wealth of these families from being shared across more and more people as it passed from one generation to the next.

These laws meant that this land and wealth remained unshared across the generations, from first-born son to first-born son.

There was once a family of paint manufacturers. They also helped the rulers of the same country fight wars in other countries. (Although they were not made into aristocrats.)

■

The family of paint manufacturers have a daughter, let's call her *Daughter A*.

The first family of aristocratic landowners have a son. Let's call him: *Landowning Heir Number 1*.

■

The Landowning Heir Number 1 and Daughter A marry. At the time of their wedding, she is twenty-two years old and he is forty-six.

They rent a house with ten bedrooms. This house belongs to the monarch of their country and is situated on one of the monarch's estates.

It is called Park House.

■

In the first eight years of marriage, they have three children: two daughters and then a boy.

Daughter A's second daughter is said to be very beautiful, let's call her *Daughter B*.

■

The other aristocratic landowning family have a son, let's call him *Landowning Heir Number 2*.

Landowning Heir Number 2 starts a romantic relationship with Daughter B. She is seventeen years old, and still at school, and he is twenty-nine.

Daughter A, Daughter B's mother, encourages the relationship.

■

Three years later, Daughter B and Landowning Heir Number 2 marry. Their wedding is held in their country's most important religious building. It is attended by over 1,500 guests, including the monarch of their country.

The details of Daughter B's wedding are published in the newspapers of their country.

■

The Landowning Heir Number 2 has not yet inherited his family's estate.

So, after two years, they move into Park House.

■

In the first year of marriage, Daughter B gives birth to a daughter.

In the third year of marriage, Daughter B gives birth to a daughter.

In the sixth year of marriage, Daughter B gives birth to a son, who dies ten hours after his birth.

■

Many years later, Daughter B will say that she was left alone for hours after giving birth.

Many years later, Daughter B will say that her son was taken away from her as soon as he was born.

Many years later, Daughter B will say that the door to her room in Park House was locked and when she banged on the door nobody came.

Many years later, Daughter B will say that she was never allowed to see or hold her son.

Many years later, Daughter B will say that this was decided by Daughter A and Landowning Heir Number 2.

■

The death certificate of Daughter B's son lists 'extensive malformation' as his cause of death.

Daughter A and the Landowning Heir Number 2 send Daughter B to the city for gynaecological examinations by multiple doctors. The stated purpose of these examinations is to determine what is wrong with Daughter B; why can she produce daughters who survive, but not sons?

■

In the seventh year of marriage, Daughter B has a miscarriage.

In the eighth year of marriage, Daughter B gives birth to a daughter, let's call her *Daughter C.*

In the tenth year of marriage, Daughter B gives birth to a son, her last child. She is twenty-eight years old.

■

As an adult, Daughter B's third daughter, Daughter C, will recall hiding behind a door as the Landowning Heir Number 2 assaults Daughter B, slapping Daughter B's face while Daughter B cries.

There was once a family of wealthy wallpaper manufacturers. For a while this family spent some time in a country that had been a faraway colony of the country of the families of aristocratic landowners.

The family of wealthy wallpaper manufacturers have a son. Let's call him the *Wallpaper Heir*.

■

In the twelfth year of marriage, Daughter B begins a relationship with the Wallpaper Heir. At the time, she is thirty-one years old and he is forty-one.

The Wallpaper Heir is married.

■

Daughter B and the Landowning Heir Number 2 agree to separate. They agree that Daughter B will leave Park House with her two youngest children (her other two children are living at their school).

■

Daughter B moves to the city. She takes her two youngest children with her. They go to school in the city, and visit the Landowning Heir Number 2 at weekends.

■

Daughter B and her two youngest children return to Park House to celebrate the main religious holiday of their country with the Landowning Heir Number 2.

During this visit, Daughter B asks the Landowning Heir Number 2 for a divorce.

The Landowning Heir Number 2 refuses to let the two youngest children return with Daughter B to the city.

■

Many years later, Daughter B will say that, two weeks after the main religious holiday of their country, she returned to Park House for her children, but she was not allowed to enter. She will say that she shouted for her children but they did not hear her.

Daughter B sues the Landowning Heir Number 2 for custody of her children.

The Landowning Heir Number 2 argues that Daughter B is not a fit mother.

Daughter A testifies against Daughter B.

■

At the time in this country, a court could only grant a divorce for certain reasons. These reasons include adultery and cruelty.

■

The Wallpaper Heir and his wife divorce. The court grants the divorce on the grounds of adultery, specifically, the Heir to Family of the Wealthy Wallpaper Manufacturer's relationship with Daughter B.

The details of the Wallpaper Heir's divorce are published in the newspapers of their country during the last days of Daughter B's custody hearing.

■

Daughter B loses custody of her four surviving children.

Daughter B sues for divorce from the Landowning Heir Number 2. The reason she gives is cruelty.

The Landowning Heir Number 2 sues for divorce from Daughter B. The reason he gives is adultery, specifically, Daughter B's relationship with the Wallpaper Heir.

■

The court grants the divorce on the grounds of adultery, specifically, Daughter B's relationship with the Wallpaper Heir.

The details of Daughter B's divorce are published in newspapers of their country.

■

Two years later, Daughter B sues for custody of her children again. She is unsuccessful.

Whether the Landowning Heir Number 2 or any of the other people involved were bad people doesn't interest me. We're all capable of doing harm and being harmed; in that sense he's the same as anyone else.

For example, approximately twenty years before the evening when, according to his daughter, he assaulted Daughter B, Landowning Heir Number 2 participated in a war on behalf of his country during which, according to his surviving son, he watched as his best friend was shot in the head and died.

We don't know whether, or to what extent, this contributed to his behaviour towards Daughter B. If we assume it did, and if we assume the accounts of Daughter B and her third daughter are true, then the Landowning Heir Number 2 did something that many men who have fought in wars on behalf of their countries have done: reproduce violence experienced at war in his own home as domestic violence. We're all capable of being harmed and doing harm.

The difference is the landowning.

Large age gaps in relationships are not necessarily a moral problem. The problem here is how young Daughter A and Daughter B were and the reproductive toll on their bodies. Both Daughter A and Daughter B stopped having children once they had given birth to sons who survived, new heirs to the aristocratic, landowning families.

Why did the aristocratic landowning families need heirs? So that, over time, the land and other wealth of their families would not be shared, even among their own children.

For Daughter B, this meant she would have six pregnancies, one miscarriage, five labours and one baby who died, between the ages of eighteen and twenty-eight years old.

Some questions I have:

Who works the land? Who lives on the land? Who owns the land?

Who creates the wealth? Who gets the wealth?

Who is beating their wives?

And what is the role of the monarchy and the state, in the theft of the land, the theft of the wealth, and the beating of wives?

Park House has been abandoned since 2020. It's on one of the estates of the new monarch of this country and is currently marked as 'Private' on the map on the estate's website.

I call the estate and ask if it is possible to arrange a visit to Park House. I don't even want to go inside, I say, just to look at it.

No.

I find Park House on Google Street View. I look at the tall estate wall, and then a locked metal gate. I move down the road on Google Street View. After the gate is a low brick wall with iron railings, which continues for about 200 metres. Fencing made from smooth, widely spaced wires. The entrance to a cricket club. Google Maps Satellite view shows a cricket pitch behind the Park House garden.

I get the bus from the train station to the village where my bed and breakfast is. Before arriving I worry that the bed and breakfast will have a door or gate that the owners lock at night, restricting my ability to enter and exit freely. When I arrive I speak for some time with the woman who runs the bed and breakfast about her dog. I tell the woman that I like to go running late in the evenings. She says that this is not a problem.

My period comes. I don't have painkillers, tampons, sanitary towels or my insertable cup so I cram wads of folded toilet paper into my pants and take half-hourly showers to avoid getting blood on the sheets. I play American sitcoms at a low volume on my tablet and, eventually, sleep through the pain.

When I walk up the avenue to the estate, it is lined on the outside by fully grown beech trees with grey-burgundy coloured leaves, and on the inside by beech saplings with green leaves. The lawn between the trees is pocked with molehills; a pheasant hops across it; a hedgehog lies on the avenue road flat and emptied like hedgehog glove. I walk parallel to the estate wall. In the gift shop there is: estate sherry, estate chutney, estate tweed; postcards of the new monarch's watercolours; pillows bearing the flag of this country; pink princess outfits for children (tiara sold separately); the faces of the old monarch and the new monarch on books, plates, tea towels and spoons.

I eat my lunch as I watch tourist families eat their lunch and then I pay £23 for a ticket to the estate house and gardens. I walk around the gardens and the ornamental lakes and the church. When it begins to rain and I go inside the house, where people in uniforms explain the downstairs rooms to me: the six sofa-ed sitting room, the thirty-two-seat dining table, the gun room and the ballroom, where an exhibition of the new monarch's watercolours has recently been installed.

In the bathroom of the café on the estate grounds, where the new monarch's collection of antique cars is on display, I replace the wad of toilet paper in my pants. I go back to the bed and breakfast; lie on the bed. I eat a curry in a pub garden, surrounded by rabbits.

It keeps raining. Light, warm rain. It settles on the outside of my jumper, which I have knitted myself; something that makes me feel calm, self-sufficient and complete, as if I can create beauty and functional clothing almost all by myself. Muntjac appear. I film them on my phone.

Daughter C, the third daughter, the one who as an adult will recall hiding behind a door, watching as her father slaps her mother as her mother cries, is called Diana.

I slip between the smooth, widely spaced wires. I climb over the brick wall and its iron railings and approach the house through clouds of bracken and rhododendron small like a child, knees scratched by brambles, thighs in the nettles, feet in the touch-me-nots along the ground.

I walk down the dark mud drive of the cricket club next door, cross the empty cricket pitch and step comfortably over the stile up to my waist in lavender and the white grass of the untended garden of the house.

I look through its windows. I stand outside the door. I greet the bees and then I stay until dark, removing clothes with the night. I cross my ankles, arse against the earth, and I thank god I am not pregnant. To celebrate, I drink sweet shoplifted sherry. I spark a blunt. I swim among the bracken and the rhododendron inside a firmament of bird sound. I masturbate to the moon.

Rich Things

CHITRA RAMASWAMY

1. Urban Oasis

The Alasdair Gray Archive is held in a small unit on the fifth floor of a former whisky bond high on a hill in north Glasgow. Inside is a feeling, like history itself, of being in a box inside a box inside a box inside a box. It is ten minutes' walk from Cowcaddens subway station, a walk through lost history that begins, as so much begins in cities, beside a motorway. I walk beneath an underpass overlooked by tall metal flowers, the last remaining evidence that a Victorian park once existed here. I ascend to the Port Dundas canal basin, past a graffitied information board titled 'Urban Oasis', which invites passers-by to 'close your eyes, ignore the traffic (if you can!)' and imagine what was here not so long ago: the 'chatter of children' from the nearby nursery and play park. The 'trickle of water springing from a decorative fountain'.

The whisky bond, which comes into sight as soon as I reach the canalside, is built as a bonded warehouse for Highland Distilleries in 1957.

This is when the park is cleared to make way for Scotland's busiest motorway: the M8.

This is when Alasdair Gray graduates from Glasgow School of Art with a diploma in Design and Mural Painting.

This is when Alasdair Gray, Artist, appears.

In the 1970s, the decade housing my birth, the building becomes a mushroom factory.

Whisky and mushrooms.

Distillation and sprouting.

Art does both.

2. Your desk

You found your desk on the side of a street, where you often picked up old things. You liked to find a new use for them. The desk is large, wooden, and has only two legs, so is drilled directly into the whitewashed walls of the whisky bond. You must have come across it in the 1970s because inside, on the lid's scuffed white underside, you portioned the space into a grid of small squares, and out of almost nothing made yourself a 1976 diary. Most of the squares you never filled – we have this tendency in common – but in a few you scribbled tantalising notes. Like:

Liz Lochhead

Christmas Day

Leave for Pitlochry

This is all I know of the story of your desk.

In *Recollections of My Nonexistence*, Rebecca Solnit tells the genesis story of her desk. It was given to Solnit by a friend who was stabbed fifteen times by an ex-boyfriend as her punishment for leaving him. The story of Solnit's desk, where she found and eventually began to use her writer's voice, is one of violence against her gender. And mine. 'Now I wonder,' writes Solnit, 'if everything I have ever written is a counterweight to that attempt to reduce a young woman to nothing.'

The things that enter our lives tell our stories, and the stories of the world.

You knew this, Alasdair.

And now I am writing these hard-won words at your desk.

3. Your ledger

The ledger you found in a skip in the 1960s came from an accountancy firm whose entries in blue ink you wrote and sketched around. This is a metaphor for how you worked: beginning with what was already there. Working around, mapping over, distorting, and making your own version.

The ledger is an archive of your mind.

It is filled with:

Diary entries, which, like most, begin with a promise to write little and often, collecting 'upon these pages all the practical, fanatical, and obsessive threads of your life at this point,' and soon peter out.

Repetitions of strange and magnetic phrases, such as 'He has wounded his body in the traditional places', over and over again, on page after page.

Passages where you're figuring out sections of *Lanark*, a panorama which grew in your mind for thirty years.

Black-and-white photos of Glasgow.

Sketches referring to your largest painting, *Cowcaddens Streetscape in the Fifties*, the top right-hand corner of which shows the view from the archive's window: Applecross Wharf, the little bridge over the canal, the low whitewashed fronts of Scotland's oldest surviving canal buildings, and Old Basin House, now on the Buildings at Risk register.

Sketches of pylons.

Newspaper clippings.

Charcoal drawings of the canal.

Postcards of Dunoon.

What I'm drawn to is the very first diary entry, written on Sunday 25 August 1963, in which you describe going shopping with your heavily pregnant wife, Inge. You go into a delicatessen in Cowcaddens, the kind that's 'fairly new to this country, certainly to Cowcaddens'. You have come into a little money and are looking, specifically, for cocktail sausages. There is only one other person in the small shop: 'a middle-aged brown leather-faced Jamaican'. When you and Inge enter, he says goodbye and leaves.

That's it.

Know this, Alasdair. Sixty years later, all the practical, fanatical and obsessive threads of my life at this point lead me here. To this Jamaican man in a deli in Cowcaddens in the summer of 1963 – four years before my father arrived in the country. For too long, I have been identifying with the wrong people. It is with this man that I stand now.

4. The green chair

The chair is high-backed, shapely, shiny armed. Immediately one knows it is a seat of knowledge. It takes pride of place in the archive, just as it did in your life. Which is also to say your work, for I understand now that work, life and love occupied the same space for you, just as your three chairs in the archive, placed as they are, appear to be in eternal conversation. It is this way for me too. Through the painstaking business of putting one word next to another today, yesterday, and virtually every other day of the last twenty years, I have built myself. It happens slowly, this becoming, like the accumulation of things in the rooms of our lives. So, there is no wall between our living and working spaces, neither in the mind nor the home. I am writing this at my kitchen table.

Winnie Wilson gifted you the chair. You used to phone her every morning to check on her, which was your less tangible but no less significant gift to her. She left most of her furnishings to you in her will. You gave most of them away but you kept the chair. And it kept you. Some people have characters so strong they rub off on things as well as people. Like the pair of shoes lined up at the door that serve as an unintended self-portrait of their owner, the green chair looks like you.

It can be traced back to your flat on Turnberry Road, then Kersland Street where you lived, wrote, painted, loved, despaired and slept in the one room in that giant council flat teeming with lodgers. All of life and life's work happened there.

The chair appeared in your life drawings.

The chair was a perch for people to observe you.

The chair was depicted as a throne in your Greenbank Church of Scotland mural.

The chair's penultimate home – and your last – was on Marchmont Terrace, which belonged to your second wife, Morag.

Now the chair is in its final resting place. Here. Along with everything else in this threatened world, it has outlasted you. Such banal facts become staggering after a death.

Some say that to sit in your green chair is the closest you can get to being Alasdair Gray.

So I sit in the chair.

And this is what settles in me . . .

Men get chairs. Throughout history, they come home from work and sit in their chairs. They have earned the money, and they have earned the rest. My father has a chair. It, too, has a sagging undercarriage and worn arms. Daddy's chair, we call it. My mother sat when she could, wherever she happened to be.

Women are always on their feet.

Women make homes.

Women don't get chairs.

Three months later, I come across your poem 'Not Striving', which you penned in the early 1970s. It is about the room in the Turnberry Road flat, where the green chair first came to live with you. The poem is about the labour that lurks behind the things that surround us. So much of this is women's work. So much of it hurts.

You wrote:

> But I fear cheerless labour lies behind every gift.
>
> It is sore getting babies out.

I stand up. It's high time I got myself a chair.

5. The art of rereading

When I first read *Poor Things* it was 1997 and I was eighteen. I thought it was about feminism.

When I next read *Poor Things* it was 2022 and I was forty-three. I thought it was about colonialism.

This is how books change us.

This is how we change books.

This is how history is archived in us, like words on a page.

6. Who gets archives

It is harder for an immigrant to have an archive.

And almost impossible for a refugee.

7. Who takes archives

I learned recently that the British stole so much over centuries of empire that 'lut', which is Hindi for 'spoils of war', entered the English language as 'loot.'

English is my language.

This is how I wield it now.

8. Glasgow is a magnificent city

You and I never met. But in 1997 – my first year at Glasgow University – you came to one of my English literature lectures. In the brutalist Boyd Orr building, you – the great Alasdair Gray, author of *Lanark* and a book called *Poor Things* I was supposed to be reading – spoke to us of things I have forgotten. I do recall the perspective: sitting high up in that steep-sided, strip-lit amphitheatre of a room, where the mischief-makers tend to flock. You were faraway, fluffy headed, with a big round paunch stretched over a dark jumper. You were impish, cantankerous, gruff, seemingly drunk. Towards the end of the lecture a student on my right put up their hand and asked you an earnest question about intertextuality in *Poor Things*.

You looked up at them and roared: 'Intertextuality? Fuck intertextuality!'

This is the moment that crystallises in my memory. A memory I will carry carelessly, like a penny in a pocket, for the next twenty-six years. Until I retrieve it. Write it down. Use it. Today.

You were what I had always wanted to be. A writer. You had written your own books and could say whatever you liked about them. About intertextuality. About Glasgow. About yourself. You were possibility.

On page 243 of *Lanark* – that glorious passage that those who love you, and this city, have seized for themselves – Thaw and McAlpin look across the city and imagine it into a new form of existence.

'Glasgow is a magnificent city,' McAlpin says. 'Why do we hardly ever notice that?'

'Because nobody imagines living here,' Thaw replies.

In Glasgow I became a writer. Only now, a quarter of a century later, do I fully appreciate that the view out of the window is that same terrain. Literally, and imaginatively. And so, on my last day in your archive, I walk into the view facing west. Over the 'shallow arch of a wooden bridge' that Thaw and McAlpin use to cross the canal. Beyond it lies the 'threadbare green hill' where, at the top, they stand under an electric pylon and survey Glasgow.

So I climb up there.

Stand under the pylon.

Survey Glasgow.

You wrote that if a city hasn't been used by an artist, not even the inhabitants live there imaginatively.

Which leads me here

to this very thought

on this very hill.

If a person hasn't been described by a writer they can't inhabit themselves imaginatively either.

Here, now, I'm on my way.

The above is an extract from a longer work produced by the author in the autumn and winter of 2022, in response to a commission from the Alasdair Gray Archive and in collaboration with the creative writing department at the University of Strathclyde. The brief was to make new work inspired by or responding to the Alasdair Gray Archive, established in March 2020, three months after Gray's death.

To Seem the Stranger

SEÁN HEWITT

Both anniversaries of my father's death have fallen on the weekend of Pride in Dublin. Each year the contrast is difficult and stark. In 2021 Pride returned to an in-person event – the city was decked with flags for the march (or parade, depending on your view of the event's relationship to corporate sponsorship). In the evening there was the heavy bass of the massive block party at the local Museum barracks, and the bars and pubs on Capel Street spilled over with colourful people from early in the afternoon. I recognise the trope: a summer day, everyone happy and celebratory, and the mourner at home, hurt that the world outside doesn't mirror their own situation. The strain that this coincidence put on my relationship to community made the pain more complicated, having the celebration of both a shared and a personal history land on the most difficult day of my year.

When I woke on the morning of the second anniversary I already felt drained. I wanted to create an inviolable haven of memory and melancholy to inhabit: I played my father's records (Cat Stevens, mostly, on a loop), cried, felt isolated not just from those around me and from the festivities of the city, but from my father and my family, 150 miles away, in England. Early in the morning my mother sent me a photograph of his grave: full of flowers, the graveyard lush and green as it was on the day of his funeral, and I was pained by the feeling of separation, not just between my father and me (one dead, the other alive), but also between my father's body, his grave across the sea, and myself in Dublin. I felt a doubled anxiety.

My boyfriend asked me what I wanted to do for the day and I suggested walking to Glasnevin Cemetery on Dublin's north side. At least I would be in a graveyard, even if it wasn't the right graveyard. The day was close and overcast, and we took a route avoiding the city centre: through the Phoenix Park, along the South Circular Road and then northwards along the backstreets. I was not in the mood to be seen.

When we reached the tall gates and walked through into the high-walled greenness of the cemetery, its imposing round tower, I felt a sort of peace or harmony between myself and the other visitors. I had decided on the walk over that I wanted to find Gerard Manley Hopkins's grave. I wanted to pay respects to *someone*, even if it was a poet-priest who had died well over a century before, even if it wasn't my father. Over the years I'd lived in Dublin, I'd become intimately obsessed with Hopkins but had still never made the pilgrimage. It felt fitting, too, that on Pride weekend, feeling isolated from the event myself, I should come to the grave of a closeted man, a man who had guided me for so long, who I felt, in that intangible way, related to.

At a petrol station across the busy dual carriageway, I bought an overpriced bouquet of ugly flowers interspersed with fake plastic ornaments, some of the foliage sprayed with glitter, and stood by a red plastic bin on the forecourt pulling out the offending stems, trying to get the bouquet into some presentable, solemn, natural appearance. It was drizzling now, and I crossed back over the road to where my boyfriend was waiting beneath one of the cemetery's watchtowers (built in the early nineteenth-century to deter bodysnatchers), his hood pulled up to block the rain.

In the Jesuit plot, Hopkins's name is carved into a stone alongside a long list of others: there is nothing personal about his grave. Still, I laid the flowers onto the monument and found that I was crying for both my father and for Hopkins, and for the linking histories that had brought me here. I thought of one of his sonnets, and my mind rewrote it as an expression of my own grief, for my father, my separation from my family, and for my intercessor, my guide.

> Father and mother dear,
> Brothers and sisters are in Christ not near
> And he my peace my parting, sword and strife.

'To seem the stranger', found in his notebooks after his death, was probably written between 1884 and 1885, when Hopkins had not long been in Dublin. It was that poem that had taken the strongest hold on me during my first year in the city.

■

When I first moved to Ireland, my mother's country, not long after my twenty-seventh birthday, I saw myself, rather morosely, as following in Hopkins's footsteps. Like me, he had lived in Liverpool and moved to Dublin to take up work as a junior academic. He was given a small room at 86 St Stephen's Green, once Dublin's Catholic University, and was overworked, under-appreciated and prone to ill health. I was also junior academic, and I was also in a less-than-ideal mindset for being uprooted into a city I did not know, not least a city whose extortionate and chronically ill-regulated housing market makes it like living on quicksand at the best of times. In Liverpool, a much cheaper city, there had been space for leisure and community; in Dublin, I found, there was none. There is little space for a quiet mind in a world of precarity: any spare moment is given over if not to work, then to worrying about money. But really, 'money' doesn't cover it: worrying about money was also worrying about life, about stability, about the future, about self-worth.

At the same time, I had left behind a different state of precarity. In the relationship I had been in for years, because of my boyfriend's severe mental health difficulties, I had felt myself called on, repeatedly, to avert the death by suicide of the person I loved. I had lived the majority of my twenties under the persistent terror of failing in that duty. Now, even though that relationship was over, the terror remained: the trauma persisted beyond its cause. In a moment, I might be suddenly defensive, frightened, easily triggered into physical symptoms: cold sweats, a rapid heart rate, a white panic and self-loathing, a churning and untethered fear that I would fail in my duty to others.

So perhaps it was exactly right that I was embarking on a study of Gerard Manley Hopkins: himself, when he lived in Dublin, depressed, anxious, existentially embattled. 'To seem the stranger lies my lot, my life / Among strangèrs.' Two strangers, as any doorway into a pub in Dublin's Temple Bar could tell you, might come to make two friends.

■

I had arrived as a researcher, beginning a new project that involved work on Hopkins's study of skyscapes. Though they were not the object of my study, I became transfixed by the so-called Terrible Sonnets, written in Dublin in his final years.

One January night, after a day in the library, I cycled back through the city centre, across the Liffey, and picked up some wine from the off-licence near my house. I went inside, up to the small room I was renting out, closed the door and lay on the bed. Because I had just one or two friends in the city, and was alien to it, I felt terrifyingly alone in my sadness. That night, I drank my way quickly through the wine and, when I was dazed enough by it, I opened up my copy of Hopkins's poems and went straight to the darkest places of his work. I read 'To Seem the Stranger' in order to make myself cry: I found that it hooked into the knotted mess of my mind and drew out a terrible thread of recognition.

I am in Ireland now; now I am at a thírd
Remove.

I gave over to him my own difficulty in expressing myself aloud. He was my spokesman now, his words the outlet for my wordlessness.

It is a bad time in one's life when one can read Hopkins's late sonnets and find in them a mirror of one's own mind. One night, about a month into my time in Dublin, a friend – witness to my spiralling – sent me a sort of prescription in the form of a text: I should go to sleep, and under no circumstances was I to read any more Hopkins for a fortnight.

■

Despite being warned, I read it repeatedly, making it a talisman of my own mind. The word 'remove' appears just twice, but it is the crux, the torture device, that the sonnet turns on. It is a poem of removes – Hopkins in Ireland was removed by nationality, by geography, from family and friends. And there is worse: he is removed from hearing, from speech, from recognition and reciprocity. I knew those removes well.

I became obsessed with one of its weird rhymes, where Hopkins chimes 'hear / me' and 'I wear- / y'. Weary (an imperfect rhyme with the previous line's 'hear') is spliced, so when I first read it, I read the word as 'wear' before I corrected myself. Still, there is this aural haunting: 'wary' and 'weary' both suggest themselves, one to the ear, the other to the eye. Being wary, being nervous or afraid or anxious, begets 'weary'. When I read it, I heard the grinding, exhausting anxiety pulling me across the line, dragging me down, wearing me out with him. In that ultimately contradictory way of the literature of despair, it comforted me by mirroring my own experience, but it also stitched me more fully into its high-pitch desperation. As much as it was a source of consolation, a missive across time, it was also an agitator of my own sense of estrangement.

■

Over my years in Dublin, from those early nights with the Terrible Sonnets, I have crossed Hopkins's ghost walking the streets, have stood silently in his old bedroom, not currently accessible to the public. The same friend who once text me to tell me to put down Hopkins for a fortnight now works at the Museum of Literature Ireland (which occupies the former Catholic University building). She let me inside one afternoon this April. I looked out of Hopkins's window over the Iveagh Gardens as it rained and felt a pitiful but peaceful sense both of union and of missed connection. As my various 'removes' have shifted, and I have come to understand more about my experience of trauma and its after-effects, I have recognised my anxieties in his, and have felt less alone being, in these strange ways, beside him: standing by his bed, at his window, in the landscapes of his writing.

When I feel baffled and frustrated at my inability to say what I mean, I am brought back to the opening line of Hopkins's sonnet:

‘to *seem* the stranger lies my lot’. This is less a fear of *being* a stranger, than of *seeming* one. It is a fear of inarticulacy:

This to hoard unheard,
Heard unheeded, leaves me a lonely began.

This, I have found, is the tyrannical anxiety of memoir: to keep a trauma unheard, unregistered, is to be cut short, to feel defensive, not understood, to be cauterised in life. Still worse, perhaps, to write it and not be heard, or, being heard, not to be heeded, to be misregistered, misdefended, misunderstood, to sprout a growth alien even to one's own intentions. To be ‘a lonely began’: to have started, to have failed to reach out, or reaching out, to have failed to make the connection or to be perceived in a way that confirms one's own darkest fears about oneself. Because I had not spoken for so long, how would my words be received? As a breaking of silence, or as a rewriting of history? The question was not just *would* I be heard, but *what* would be heard. To have sought accuracy and an empathetic bridge, and to have failed in that uncontrollable place: the mind of the reader.

Still, I have sought company in a chosen family of ghosts, none closer to my side than Hopkins. It is a fantasy, of course, this closeness, but all literary affinities are. The written word invites these dream-connections, these infatuations, these intimacies. The heart ‘breeds’ them. Hopkins cannot truly be ‘a lonely began’ so long as I hear him. I offer him my company back across the intervening years, and he offers me his.

GASPAR NOÉ'S ALL-CAPS CINEMA

ROB DOYLE

20

For my fortieth birthday my friends bought me a digital film projector. It's one of those rare gifts you don't see coming that are *exactly* what you want. I'd been talking for years about getting a projector, lamenting how, having neither a TV nor a home in which to put one, whenever I wanted to watch a film that wasn't showing in cinemas, I had little choice but to do so on my laptop (somehow, taking the logical next step and actually *buying* a projector had seemed beyond me). When it finally came, the digital projector was a life-changer, a private revolution. As my forties commenced, I began staying home every night to fill in the blank zones on an internal map titled *L'histoire du cinéma*. I also started smoking weed for the first time in two decades. The activities complemented each other wonderfully. My friends didn't see me for a while.

19

I'd long imagined that, whenever I did come to own a projector, one of the first whims I'd indulge would be to screen the whole of Gaspar Noé's filmography – a home-cinema retrospective of a favourite director whose intense, shocking, confrontational, druggy, sensorially overwhelming films had both exhilarated and distressed me for two decades. But when the projector arrived, I was all Gaspared out, having only recently immersed myself in his work to coincide with the release of his geriatric melodrama *Vortex*. After a fortnight of promiscuous home viewing, I opted instead for a Dario Argento season. I had real issues with what this sick fuck was up to – as a director Argento never met a young women he didn't want to stab, bludgeon, or garrotte, and his storylines are embarrassing shlock – but his films are visually luscious thrill-rides that nicely complemented my cannabis habit. Argento is also among Gaspar Noé's cinematic fathers, and in his eighties he crossed to the other side of the camera for a debut acting role – as the male lead in *Vortex*.

18

Like many of the artists I've loved, Noé has the air of the underdog – even if he is hardly obscure in those parts of the world where we spend our time arguing about filmmakers. Noé's background is not that of an underdog nor an art-outsider (his father is the Argentine painter Luis Felipe Noé). His strain of underdoggery is rather that of seeming never to be taken entirely seriously by the critical establishment, but snubbed as a purveyor of cheap sensationalism and shock tactics. You can see where his critics are coming from. To love Noé's films is, in a sense, to *prefer* the cheap seats. He creates mesmerising, existentialist trash – an uncommon fusion of avant-garde aesthetics and adolescent provocation. And he knows it, too. After the critical kicking he took for his fourth feature film, *Love*, Noé incorporated the derision into the promo posters for his next one. A grinning, bald Gaspar holds up a cup of LSD-laced sangria under blood-red text:

YOU DESPISED *I STAND ALONE*
YOU HATED *IRREVERSIBLE*
YOU LOATHED *ENTER THE VOID*
YOU CURSED *LOVE*
NOW TRY *CLIMAX*

17

The 'end credits' that run at the *beginning* of *Vortex* scroll from the bottom of the screen to the top rather than the other way around. This is classic Gaspar, a contrary flipping of expectations for its own sake – also one of many self-quotations in his work, in this case echoing both the dance-horror *Climax* (which is virtually a mash-up of self-quotations) and the earlier *Irreversible*. The names of the lead actors and the director appear along with the years of their birth, as if on a gravestone: FRANCOISE LEBRUN 1944,

DARIO ARGENTO 1940, ALEX LUTZ 1978 and, finally, GASPAR NOE 1963. Instinctively we wonder what the absent, terminal dates will read. There is a dedication: 'To all those whose brains will deteriorate before their hearts'. Then the screen is filled with the face of the singer Françoise Hardy – one of the most beautiful faces of the twentieth century. She's in the absolute bloom of youth, aged, perhaps, twenty, and she's singing directly into the camera, a sad and lovely song about a rose, the coming of winter, the transience of all beauty. The song ends. Françoise Hardy's face disappears. An oily black line bleeds down the middle of the screen, creating two frames of equal proportions. In one, an old man lies in bed. In the other, an old woman, his wife, lies beside him. Split-screen: the film's chief gimmick.

16

Gimmicks in Gaspar Noé's filmography – a non-exhaustive list:

- The countdown that flashes onscreen before the intense final act of *I Stand Alone*:

  WARNING: YOU HAVE 30 SECONDS TO LEAVE
  THIS FILM SCREENING

- The 3D sex in *Love*, which adds nothing to the film. You get the impression Noé used it as bait to get the money men on side and, then, realising it was a vacuous conceit, pushed on with it regardless.

- Intertitles: those blocks of sans-serif text that appear onscreen in virtually every film he's ever made.
- The swirling camerawork in the barely endurable first half-hour of *Irreversible*, in which two men frantic with bloodlust (one played by Vincent Cassel) descend into an infernal gay sex dungeon called the Rectum in search of the man who raped one of their wives (played by Cassel's real-life wife Monica Bellucci). Together with the lurching, molten drone score – and the sub-audible, ultra-low-frequency 'Sensurround' backdrop engineered by one of the members of Daft Punk – the nauseating camerawork seems to *will* us to walk out of the cinema.
- The reverse chronology in the same film. *Irreversible* begins with a shocking act of masculine vengeance, proceeds backwards scene by scene to the brutal trauma that precipitated it, and ends in tenderness and sensuality: the innocent bliss the couple will never know again.
- The decision to film almost the entire three hours of *Enter the Void* in an overhead POV that recalls video games, the bloody aftermath scene at the end of *Taxi Driver*, and the immersive snuff films in Kathryn Bigelow's prescient 1995 cyberpunk film *Strange Days*.

15

Neither the man nor his wife in *Vortex* can be called beautiful (in the credits they are named only as 'lui' and 'lei', him and her). Far past their summertime, their bodies and faces are heavy, grey, drained of sex and vitality. The contrast with the radiantly youthful face of Françoise Hardy could not be starker – we are plunged, immediately and characteristically, into the cinema of *obviousness*. The old woman is played by Françoise Lebrun, who, in her youth, starred in Jean Eustache's 1973 film *The Mother and the Whore* (a film beloved by Gaspar). Noé is one of those directors who flaunts his cinephilia, recurrently paying tribute to his idols. His reverence for Kubrick's *2001: a Space Odyssey* is near religious. On his soundtracks he appropriates scores from trash cinema of the past, while film posters adorn the walls of his characters' homes (Gaspar has suggested that he owns the world's largest collection of film posters). Murphy, *Love*'s aspiring-filmmaker protagonist, wears a T-shirt emblazoned with the word 'Fassbinder'. In *Vortex*, Dario Argento plays a film scholar who is writing a book about dreams and cinema titled 'Psyche'. We watch him watching films and attending a meeting of fellow cineastes who collectively publish a film magazine. In a press interview, Argento recounts how a young Noé approached him at the Cannes Film Festival in the early 1990s, declaring himself a devotee and inviting his hero to a screening of his film *Carne*. 'There was something in this kid's eyes,' Argento said, 'so I went to see his film.' They've been friends ever since.

14

There's something in the elderly woman's eyes, too. I take back what I said above: she *is* beautiful, and that's where it is, in the eyes. But her beauty is also in her frailty. Her husband is still asleep beside her but she's awake, peering around the room – we realise she's bewildered, frightened. She doesn't know where, perhaps even *who* she is. She clutches her husband's body, which is turned on its side. Does she even recognise him? Or is she in bed with a stranger in a strange house, the familiar made alien through the havoc wreaked by dementia? What transfigures her – what makes her beautiful – is our pity. She is our mother, our wife, our lover, ourselves. We're moved not by Françoise Lebrun's performance but by that in her which is *not* performing.

13

I see Noé's influence everywhere, or imagine I do. Every nightclub scene or use of swirling or overhead camerawork; every scene where a face gets smashed in or where psychedelia is wedded to cinematography – therein lurks Gaspar. I, too, have tried to open myself to his influence, in my modest contributions to moviemaking. When the actor and director Eoin Macken optioned my novel *Here Are the Young Men*, he enlisted me to co-write the screenplay. I tried for a while, but I was tired of that story. We both agreed it was better if Macken wrote the whole thing, and from that point on my input boiled down to urging him, in sporadic emails and video calls, to make it *more like Gaspar Noé!* When the film was finally released, Noé's influence was evident in just one sequence – perhaps the film's strongest and certainly its most uncomfortable. Matthew, Kearney and Jen, three teenage friends, are together at a house party. They drink shots, take drugs. Jen and Matthew, who have recently hooked up after a slow-burning attraction, have a lovers' row. Later, Jen passes out in a bedroom at the end of a corridor. Kearney, a malevolent sadist, finds her there, sees the state she's in, and tries to rape her. As he does, Matthew staggers up the stairway and along the corridor. Red light strobes as a gnarly acid-house track pounds on the soundtrack. Slumping outside the bedroom door, Matthew witnesses his best friend kissing his girl. Kearney shuts the door in his face. Matthew crawls away and vomits in the toilet. It's almost too cruel to watch. It's pure Gaspar.

12

The first Noé film I ever saw was *Irreversible*, his second feature and still his most notorious. It came out in 2003, when I was twenty-one. My friends and I were buzzed to see this film, which was said to be brutal, shocking, unwatchable – as Noé well knows, nothing gets people flocking into cinemas like reports of mass walkouts. Even in the interests of writing this critical appreciation, I almost couldn't bring myself to rewatch *Irreversible*. At forty, my taste for the transgressive is not what it was. And yet, viewed these many years later, it's still an extraordinary – if invidiously unpleasant – film. I'd forgotten about the sinister prelude in which the butcher from *I Stand Alone* sits near-naked on a prison-cell cot, speaking with another middle-aged man. 'Time destroys everything,' he says, enacting Noé's habit of philosophical sloganeering. He confesses to the incestuous offence that landed him behind bars, prompting his cellmate to insist that 'there are no crimes, only actions' – which sounds a lot like Nietzsche's 'there are no moral facts, only interpretations'. The oppressive drone score now carries us above the scene unfolding outside the prison: a man is being carried on a stretcher out of a nightclub – the Rectum – while another man is being put under arrest. Sirens flash, cops bustle, bystanders gawk. The scene strongly references the aforementioned aftermath scene in *Taxi Driver* (Noé has claimed that if there's one movie character he wishes he could be, it's Travis Bickle) – but it also seems to reference *ahead* (aptly for a film with a reverse chronology) to *Enter the Void*, released six years later, which would expand the ambience, camerawork and sound design of this scene into a three-hour, psychedelic limit-experience. Next, the two men we've just observed are hurriedly descending into a claustrophobic gay BDSM nightclub in pursuit of a man named La Tenia – the Tapeworm. As they penetrate deeper into the Rectum, the warped, malevolent droning is gradually submerged by a frenetic industrial-techno beat. Vincent Cassel's character, Marcus, remarks that the place stinks of shit – there's no doubt that if Noé had had access to some gimmick technology that could waft faecal odour into theatres at this point, he'd have used it. The harness-strapped men groaning like tortured souls in hell as they fist, fuck and suck one another in the swirling shadows fascinated and disturbed me aged twenty-one – and they still do, only now their underworld is familiar to me. The gut-tingling cocktail of dread, excitement and aesthetic wonder I experienced when I started going regularly to Berlin nightclubs in my thirties – Berghain, in particular, with its attached gay dungeon, Laboratory – was provoked, in part, I realise now, by unconsciously recognising this realm from Noé's infernal film. Rewatching it at forty, I saw no need to subject myself to the gratuitously long, savage beating-and-rape scene. While it was projecting on the bedroom wall I went into an adjacent room to play with the cat. I could hear Monica Bellucci's screams as Sooty arched her neck to let me stroke her below her chin, the way she likes it.

11

It's perhaps inevitable that a shock artist like Noé would eventually make a film that focuses on the chaotic indignities of old age and the reality of dying (DEATH IS AN EXTRAORDINARY EXPERIENCE, declares an intertitle in *Climax*). His films directly preceding *Vortex* fixated shamelessly on nubile bodies and sexual glamour, depicting strippers, dancers, lovers and the monosyllabic fuckboys who pursue them. In Noé's world, walls throb with hard techno beats from adjacent rooms and everyone is horny and depraved, their motives baldly stated in the name of the strip club in *Enter the Void*: SEX-MONEY-POWER. Few filmmakers more vigorously inhabit what feminist theorists like to call the male gaze. His films taunt us by insisting *this is what men want when you strip away the impostures of civilisation* – not so much a rebuttal to feminists as a confirmation of their darkest suspicions. Desire is served up raw, red and unadorned like the steaks Noé orders, with a showman's flair, whenever journalists interview him in restaurants. But even the lustiest male gaze wilts before the base truth of all flesh: it ages, sags, dies, rots. Noé's macho artist's morality finally compelled him to pass from the hot summer of life – the long, sultry threesome in *Love* – to its stark and barren winter. The only remotely erotic act in *Vortex* occurs when the elderly woman, her senile synapses misfiring, awkwardly tries to kiss her adult son on the mouth (another self-quotation: in *Enter the Void*, the vulnerable Linda tries to kiss her brother Oscar while high on drugs). The film's unavoidable point of comparison – and an acknowledged inspiration – is Michael Haneke's *Amour*. Curious, how both *auteurs* of confrontation wound up making films about elderly couples staring into extinction from their Paris apartments. Having spent their working lives smugly forcing audiences to look at what hurts them (like the maniac in Dario Argento's *Opera* who inserts needles under his victim's eyelids as he butchers her loved ones), both filmmakers finally turned their (male) gaze against themselves – meticulously envisioning their own, inescapable fate.

10

Actually, the focus on decrepitude in *Vortex* isn't entirely new, but rather sees Noé come full circle. In *I Stand Alone*, his first feature film, the nameless butcher's nihilist revolt of hate, violence and incest is preceded by his taking a job at an old person's home. There, he observes an elderly woman in her final moments alive. Confused and delusional, she cries out to her father (surely long dead) not to abandon her, then describes an enveloping darkness. A typically bludgeoning intertitle reads, DEATH OPENS NO DOORS. Released in 1998, *I Stand Alone* is drenched in the twentieth-century's existentialist *machismo*, its caustic voiceover spewing a hard man's philosophy of materialist despair and brutal reductiveness. The film's title flags the antiheroic, lone-wolf fantasy of being separate from the others, independent of networks and community. Released from prison after assaulting a man he falsely believed raped his daughter, the butcher tries to rebuild his life in a grim and impoverished France (with its depiction of poverty, unemployment and a humiliated underclass bent on revenge, *I Stand Alone* veers closer to social commentary than Noé's subsequent work). Pacing the mean streets and sullen bars of Lille and Paris, always alone in the frame as if he's the last living man, the butcher calls it as he sees it: people are animals, bodies are meat, death is absolute and banal, every man stands alone, life is a war of all against all, it's fuck or be fucked, kill or be killed, even having children won't save you, they're just parasites who'll hate you and then lock you away in an old folk's home, we're totally isolated and each life is a tunnel, a long dark tunnel like the one where the parents die in a car wreck in *Enter the Void*, or the one with stark red walls in *Irreversible* where the rape takes place, or the other tunnels and orifices in Noé's films – vaginal passageways, rectal corridors, birth canals, DMT wormholes, vortices.

9

Released in 1991 and a little under forty minutes long, *Carne* also stars a sullen, middle-aged Philippe Nahon as the butcher, and, like *I Stand Alone*, boasts an urgent, martial score. This is the antihero's mean and nasty backstory – how he made a living as a horse butcher, resisting forbidden urges towards his daughter until an act of violence put him in prison. Living up to its title, *Carne* also reduces human life to the bare facts of flesh and fucking. 'Because of a nine-second orgasm, a child has to sweat for sixty years,' the butcher muses after knocking up the same barmaid who, in *I Stand Alone*, he'll pummel with his fists till he causes her to miscarry. In the seven-year gap between short and feature, no tonal, philosophical or thematic development has occurred whatsoever. Noé would remain a swaggering brutalist well into middle age. Arguably, he only really grew up two decades after his first feature, with *Vortex*. Arguably, he never grew up. The heaviest charge to be levelled at him is philosophical banality, his prideful attachment to a crudely misanthropic materialism that might have been merely a stage he passed through en route to richer philosophical horizons.

And yet it's precisely this dogged refusal to look up from the gutter that, over the long haul of his life in film, has enabled Noé to access truths of living and dying that are at once extreme and universal – the blood and shit, sperm and tears, pain and viscera that smear our being-in-the-world.

8

There's one philosophical theme in his work that *isn't* banal any more than it is (or needs to be) original. At the very beginning of *Vortex* – this happens even before Françoise Hardy sings – the couple sit on the balcony of their cluttered flat to enjoy a light meal and a glass of wine. The scene is wistful, dreamlike. The pink of the old man's shirt rhymes with the flowers along the ledge. Both of them smile, they are tender to one another. The screen has not yet split into twin isolating frames – this is their last moment happy together. As they sip their wine, the woman says, 'Life is a dream, isn't it.' 'Yes,' the old man replies, 'life is a dream within a dream.' The illusory nature of life; dreams within dreams – Noé is doing what artists do and expressing anew the perennial verities: in this case, the insubstantiality and transience of existence, which clearly has been preoccupying him lately. At the time of writing, Noé is in his late fifties. A visual poet of youth, hedonism, sensation, sex and the night, his thoughts are turning to the party's end (the tagline on *Vortex*'s promotional poster reads, 'Life is a short party that will soon be forgotten'). In 2020, just before the Covid lockdowns, Noé suffered a brain haemorrhage he was lucky to survive. His mother died in 2012 after suffering from dementia: his family's experiences of caring for her provide the film's autobiographical basis. But already with *Enter the Void* in 2009 – which was inspired by *The Tibetan Book of the Dead* – Noé seemed attuned to life's illusory character. First seeded as a line of dialogue in *I Stand Alone* – 'How quickly life passes, and all for nothing' – by the release of *Climax* in 2018, this Buddhist-Hindu-Schopenhauerian sense of life's intangibility was present as a fixation. As a dance troupe descends into horror and depravity at a cabin in the mountains after their punch is spiked with LSD, an intertitle declares: EXISTENCE IS A FLEETING ILLUSION. While it's among his more superficial films, *Climax* is haunted by the themes of transience and unreality that *Vortex*, in a more somber, adult manner, would directly confront.

7

Although his films are frequently, egoistically self-referential – the drug dealer named Gaspar in *Enter the Void*, etc. – *Vortex* and *Love* are his only autobiographical films. *Love* came out while I was living in a shabby flat in Paris's nineteenth arrondissiment. It was Noé's first feature film since *Enter the Void* had left me astounded when I saw it premiere in Dalston's Rio cinema six years earlier (with Noé himself in attendance). In the press, *Love* was described as a '3D porno'. (While he didn't seem to mind the label, Gaspar pointed out that, unlike his film, in porn there's no real emotion and women never mention pregnancy or have their period.) In my Parisian loneliness I'd eagerly awaited the film and assumed that there'd be opening night queues around the block. As it happened, I sat alone in a near-empty cinema, goofy 3D glasses on, like a sad wanker (or like Noé's abject cameo in *Irreversible*, masturbating in a sex dungeon).

6

Love was met with a fair amount of critical derision. And it *is* ridiculous, not least when the melodrama is interrupted by a towering 3D cock (that of actor Karl Glusman) spurting jizz straight at the audience; or when we watch from inside a vagina as it's being penetrated (more self-quotation here – Gaspar first pulled the pussy-POV stunt in *Enter the Void*). All this stuff is glaringly juvenile – a word, like 'visceral', that's always on the tip of the tongue in discussions of Noé – but the film as a whole is even more regressive than that: it's *infantile*, a baptismal dunk into the screaming-baby emotions, abandonment anxiety and verbal expression so blunt it's *pre*-verbal, a primal eloquence of grunts, moans, sighs, gasps and sobs. (The actual dialogue is only marginally more articulate: 'You piece of shit. PIECE OF *SHIIIIIT*!' 'I'm not a slave to pussy . . . Pussy's pussy.' 'A dick has no brain. A dick has only one purpose: to fuck. And I fucked it all up.' 'Love is strange . . . How can something so wonderful bring such great pain?') This regressiveness is the fount of the film's emotional power – I've seen it perhaps six times and I always find it movingly intimate, tender, sad and honest. But it's also aggressively carnal, a film that throbs, twitches and drips with cock and cunt, tits and bums, jizz and juice and sweat and tears – a sex-tape weepie jerking us back to a condition of raw agony and intense gratification. Some mocked it for how the characters speak in clanging clichés – and they do – but for me this was to miss the point, which is that falling in love is to be helplessly reduced to a condition of *pure* cliché, a madness of unoriginality . . . 'I love you' being the biggest cliché of them all.

5

It's in *Love* that Noé really indulges his aforementioned habit of metafictional self-reference. As the film begins, student filmmaker Murphy is glumly cohabiting with sexy Omi and their infant boy . . . Gaspar. Adorning the couple's bedroom is a neon model of the 'LOVE Hotel' from the climactic scene in *Enter the Void* (adding yet another meta layer, the *replica* hotel is *also* in *Enter the Void*). The model is like a doorway leading between one film and the other, as if Noé's oeuvre is a glittering psychedelic funhouse constructed to mirror the dimensions of his cinema-soaked psyche. Later, during a long sequence of flashbacks, Murphy's girlfriend Electra takes him to the 'Noé Art Gallery' owned by her ex – played by Gaspar himself. Electra reassures Murphy that it's completely over between her and the gallerist in an exchange that goads the audience with the spectre of unacceptable age difference:

'He left me. He was old but he wanted younger.'

'Younger than *you*?'

'Yes.'

At the gallery, Noé (wearing a fetching silver wig) treats Murphy with cursory politeness, then whisks Electra away with a promise to introduce her to influential men (she's an artist on the make). Murphy later learns that Electra has been cheating on him with Noé. At a party he drunkenly confronts Noé and smashes a champagne glass over his head. This mad sequence is remarkable for a number of reasons, chief among them being that it depicts Gaspar Noé essentially *cuckolding himself from the future* (Murphy, remember, is an autofictional protagonist), while simultaneously watching his beloved be seduced by a powerful older man *who is also himself.* It gets weirder. Murphy spends the night in a police cell where, amid stark red lighting and lurid montage with electro-funk blaring on the soundtrack, a semi-erect, blushing red cock is waved in our faces – visually echoing the finger Noé pointed at the camera moments earlier. I've always suspected that this really is Gaspar Noé's cock. Next, we see Noé fucking Electra from behind – the older gallerist/director establishing dominance over his young masculine rival in the most literal way. Are the actors fucking for real, the director going at it with his young female lead? The rest of the film's sex is unsimulated, so we wouldn't bet against it.

4

What is it with Noé and babies? With Noé and mothers? In *Love* Gaspar names a baby after himself, while across his films grown men and women curl up like foetuses, desolate and vulnerable. *Enter the Void* depicts a foetus being aborted. In *I Stand Alone* the butcher punches his pregnant girlfriend's belly, killing their unborn child. In *Climax* a pregnant woman is also punched in the belly, while another woman locks her little boy inside a maintenance room, where he is attacked by rats and electrocuted. In *Carne*, real-life footage of a baby being pulled out of its mother's body is juxtaposed with the graphic slaughter of a horse. Violence against babies, wombs, women, foetuses . . . We needn't subscribe to all of Sigmund Freud or Melanie Klein to suspect that Gaspar is symbolically brutalising himself, pounding on the tiny, swaddled shell of his own fragility and dramatising – even as he intensifies – the coarsening of his finer sensibilities. Gaspar is the butcher in *I Stand Alone* who, sitting in the darkness of a porno cinema, tells himself he's like a cock that must stay hard all the time to earn respect. But Gaspar (who has described himself as a frustrated father) is also the helpless foetus, the abortion, the little boy locked inside the maintenance room screaming for his mammy – and so too are Gaspar's audiences, who consent to view these demoralising images of harm and violation.

3

Dario Argento, Gaspar's sick fuck of a father figure, stole a trick from Hitchcock by habitually filming in close up his own, gloved hands for the trademark kill scenes that pepper his *gialli*. In *Vortex*, now that the camera is turned *against* Argento, no stabbings or eviscerations are needed: the cruelty is inflicted by time itself (the climactic intertitle in *Irreversible* reads: TIME DESTROYS EVERYTHING). Wayward son Gaspar needs only point and shoot: it's torture by camera, revenge on behalf of all the pretty women Argento has maimed, stabbed, boiled or battered in his films. *Vortex* is Gaspar's Oedipal snuff movie – Argento's onscreen death of a heart attack is as awful as that of the girl in *Suspiria* who falls into a bed of barbed wire. Before killing him, Gaspar subjects Argento to a series of humiliations. The old man's wife, lost to senility but perhaps intuiting that he's been carrying on with a much younger woman named Claire, tears up his work in progress and flushes it down the toilet. The implication is brazen – *your work is shit!* If Gaspar is the son as Oedipal sadist, he is also the *guilty* son – his avatar in *Vortex* is the couple's grown-up child Stefan, played by Alex Lutz, who retreats into heroin addiction as his parents endure their final torments.

2

WHEN THE PRESSURE GETS TOO STRONG, I TURN INTO A DICTATOR, reads a quote from Rainer Werner Fassbinder in *Lux Æterna*, an ominous, stressful, semi-essayistic and extremely meta short(ish) film featuring Latin intertitles that riff on the art of filmmaking. Karl Glusman again plays a budding filmmaker (perhaps the same one he played in *Love*). Accosting Charlotte Gainsbourg on the set of a film she's acting in, he tries to talk her into starring in a film he wants to make called 'Danger' – which is the title Gaspar had in mind for the film that would eventually become *Love* (and the word that fills the screen after the countdown in *I Stand Alone*). Amidst all these meta layers there's a witchy choral soundtrack and an abundance of sacrilegious imagery – glib for a proud atheist like Gaspar – including inverted crucifixes, one of which is carved into a little girl's vagina (off-screen, mercifully). The film ends with a Latin dad joke, translated in the subtitles as: THANK GOD I'M AN ATHEIST. *Lux Æterna* is the only Gaspar Noé film I've been content to watch just once.

1

In contrast to his earlier shockers, much of *Vortex* concerns uneventful domesticity. We watch *lei et lui* making coffee, peeing, pottering about. He shuffles his printed notes and types with two fingers on a keyboard; she wanders and gets lost in the neighbourhood. For long stretches there's no dialogue. It's a bit boring, though I didn't notice this the first time I saw the film, distracted as I was by the question of which of the two panels I ought to be looking at. I kept having FOMO – my concentration never wavered but for all I knew, the real action was happening right now over the other side, on the panel I could hazily make out in my peripheral vision. What was she up to? Where was he now? The subtitles made a third claim on my attention, and amid this triangle I kept losing sight of how little there was going on, narratively speaking. *Vortex* is at base a meditation – on impermanence, sickness, old age and death – the quietest film by a director who's otherwise all noise and fury.

0

In writing this appreciation, I'd have failed to honour my subject if I didn't incorporate some sort of formal gimmick. I have no tolerance for typographical trickery – inflated or tiny text, alternating fonts, squiggly symbols and so on. Split-screen might have worked: a horizontal divide such as JM Coetzee used in his novel *Diary of a Bad Year*, with my commentary on Noé's films running above and digressions from my life as a cinemagoer below; or a vertical divide like that in *Vortex*, with all I admire in Noé's work on one plane and my reservations on the other. But in the end I opted for this countdown, so that I begin with everything and end up . . .

-1

. . . with less than nothing. 'I want to make movies out of blood, semen and tears,' says Murphy during a romantic Paris walk in *Love*, echoing what a young Gaspar no doubt told his girlfriends. Birth, copulation, impregnation, abortion, dementia, death – if you watch Noé's films in reverse order, from *Vortex* to *Carne*, you'll pass like a soul reliving its earthly existence from the silence of the funeral urn to the gore of the birthing table. But where to go next? What to make films about when you've shown us *everything*, from birth and death to *re*birth and the psychedelic hereafter? Maybe Gaspar will take his self-reflexive habits to their terminal conclusion and film his *own* death – not quietly in a hospital bed, but violently in a tunnel or a nightclub, a sensational death soundtracked by Coil or Throbbing Gristle that will trigger mass walkouts and polarise the critics. The film could be given a typically dramatic, single-word title – *Snuff*, or *Death*, or *Inferno*. Or, perhaps, having got the upward scrolling credits out of the way at the start, he'll decide to call it simply:

THE END

Notes on contributors

Chitra Ramaswamy writes for the *Guardian*, is the restaurant critic for the *Times Scotland* and broadcasts for BBC radio. She is the author of *Homelands* and *Expecting*.

Seán Hewitt is the author of *All Down Darkness Wide*, *Tongues of Fire* and *300,000 Kisses*. He was awarded the Rooney Prize for Irish Literature in 2021.

Hilary A White is a writer, arts journalist and conservationist. His work has featured in the *Dublin Review* and is forthcoming in *Winter Papers*. He is working on *The City of Hawks*, a book about raptors in the fabric of Dublin city.

Sinéad Gleeson's *Constellations* was shortlisted for the Rathbones Folio Prize and the James Tait Black Memorial Prize. Her novel, *Hagstone*, will be published in 2024.

Yara Rodrigues Fowler's first novel, *Stubborn Archivist*, was longlisted for the Dylan Thomas and the Desmond Elliot prizes. Yara's second novel, *there are more things*, was nominated for the Orwell Prize for Political Fiction and Goldsmiths Prize. In 2023, Yara was chosen as one of Granta's 'Best Young British Novelists'.

Patrick James Errington is the author of the *swailing* and the French translator of PJ Harvey's *The Hollow of the Hand*. His translation of EM Cioran's *Notebooks* will be published by New York Review Books.

EM Cioran (1911–1995) was a Romanian philosopher and aphorist who, after 1937, lived and published primarily in France. His works in French – almost all translated by Richard Howard – include *A Short History of Decay* and *The Temptation to Exist*, all originally published by Gallimard.

Ruby Eastwood is a twenty-two-year-old filmmaker and writer living in Dublin. She is currently studying for a MA and writing a novel.

Rob Doyle is the author of four books: *Threshold*, *Autobibliography*, *This Is the Ritual*, and *Here Are the Young Men*. His writing has appeared in the *New York Times*, the *Observer*, the *Dublin Review* and elsewhere.

Clare Fisher's debut novel, *All the Good Things*, won a Betty Trask Award. Their short-story collection, *How the Light Gets In*, was longlisted for the Edge Hill Short Story prize and the International Dylan Thomas Prize. Their most recent short-story collection is *The Moon Is Trending*.

Sara Baume is the author of four books, the most recent of which, *Seven Steeples*, was shortlisted for the Goldsmiths Prize and the International Dylan Thomas Prize. In 2023 she was named one of Granta's 'Best Young British Novelists'.

Conor Dawson's writing appears in the *Dublin Review*, the *Shanghai Literary Review* and elsewhere. He is currently working on a series of interlinked personal essays.

Shannan Mann is an award-winning poet whose poems have appeared (or are forthcoming) in *Poetry Daily*, *Poet Lore*, *Gulf Coast* and elsewhere. She also translates devotional and erotic Sanskrit poetry.

Liam Cagney's fiction has been published in *Winter Papers* and *gorse* and was shortlisted for the White Review Short Story Prize, and his music writing appears in the *Irish Times* and the *Guardian*.